Sri- Chakra

Its Yantra, Mantra and Tantra

Sri Garib Das Oriental Series no.333

Sri- Chakra

Its Yantra, Mantra and Tantra

S.K. Ramachandra Rao

Sri Satguru Publications

A Division of

Indian Books Centre

Delhi, India

Published by
Sri Satguru Publications,
Indological and Oriental Publishers
A Division of
Indian Books Centre
40/5, Shakti Nagar,
Delhi-110007
India

First Edition; Bangalore , 1982
Second Edition : Delhi , 2008
Reprint: 2011

ISBN 81-7030-900-9

Printed at Dynamic Printers, Delhi

Mūkāmbikā, Kollūr

।।ऐं ह्रीं श्रीं ऐं क्लीं सौः।।

कला विद्या पराशक्तिः श्रीचक्राकाररूपिणी।
तन्मन्ध्ये बैन्दवं स्थानं तत्रास्ते परमेश्वरी।।

सदाशिवेन संयुक्ता सर्वतत्वातिगामिनी।
चक्रं त्रिपुरसुन्दर्या ब्रह्माण्डाकारमोश्वरि।।

पञ्चभूतात्मकं चेव तन्मात्रात्मकमेव च।
इन्द्रियात्मकमेव च मनस्तत्त्वात्मकं तथा।।

मायादितत्त्वरूपं च तत्त्वातीतं तु बैन्दवम्।
बैन्दवे जगदुत्पत्तिस्थितिसंहारकारिणी।।

(Bhirava-yāmala)

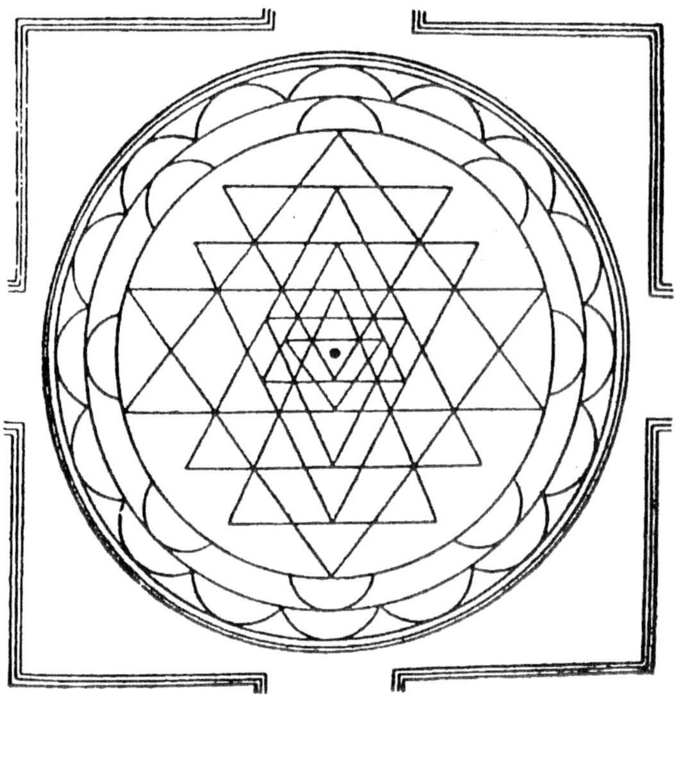

Preface

Śrī-chakra has rightly been regarded as the 'prince among *chakras*' (*chakra-rāja*). It is the best known and most worshipped among hundreds of sacred designs that are prescribed in the traditional lore. Despite this celebrity, an air of mystery surrounds this *chakra*. It is even classed among things, the knowledge of which should not be made readily available!

While there is considerable justification for not exposing our religious themes to vulgar gaze and to idle curiosity, knowledge about them needs to be made available to the earnest seekers. Details concerning Śrī-chakra have always been looked upon as precious secrets; but there have always been tracts in Sanskrit seeking to explain the details of the *chakra*, their significance, the way it is constructed and the manner of its worship. Initiation into its ceremonial worship is of course a matter of personal commitment to a competent *guru*, and must be resorted to in the ritualistic isolation that is prescribed.

The present book carefully avoids the details concerning initiation and the actual worship. They cannot become the subject-matters of a book. But the details of the design itself, the significance of those details, the philosophical framework that renders the details relevant, the prevailing symbolisms, and the nature of the source material have been explained here, based on authoritative texts and traditional understanding.

We are grateful to the Indian Books Centre for reprinting this work which has been out of pring for a long time.

Trustees

Prof. S.K.R. Memorial Trust (R)

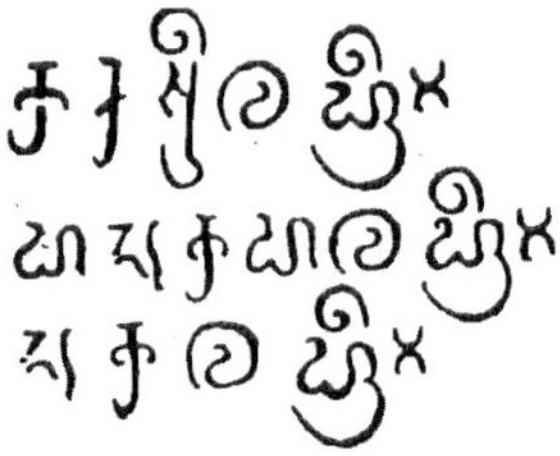

Pañcha-daśī in old *vengi* character

Pañcha-daśī in Pallava characters

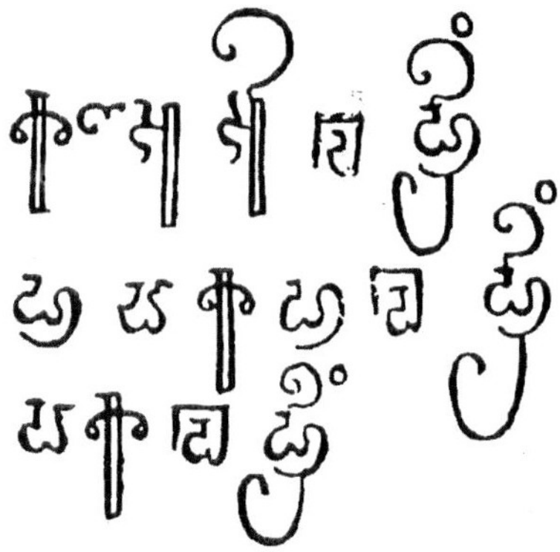

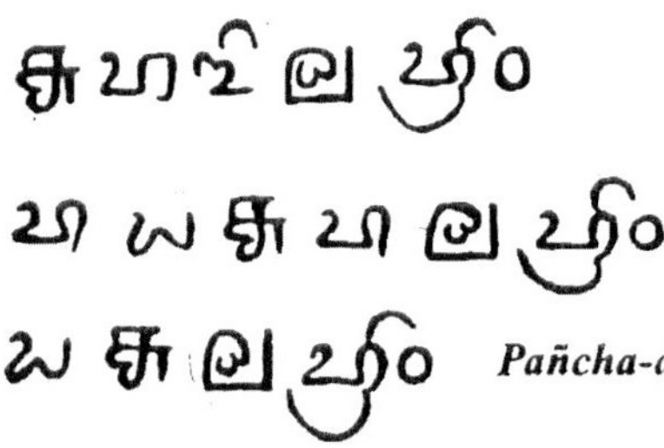

Pañcha-daśī in *grantha* characters.

Contents

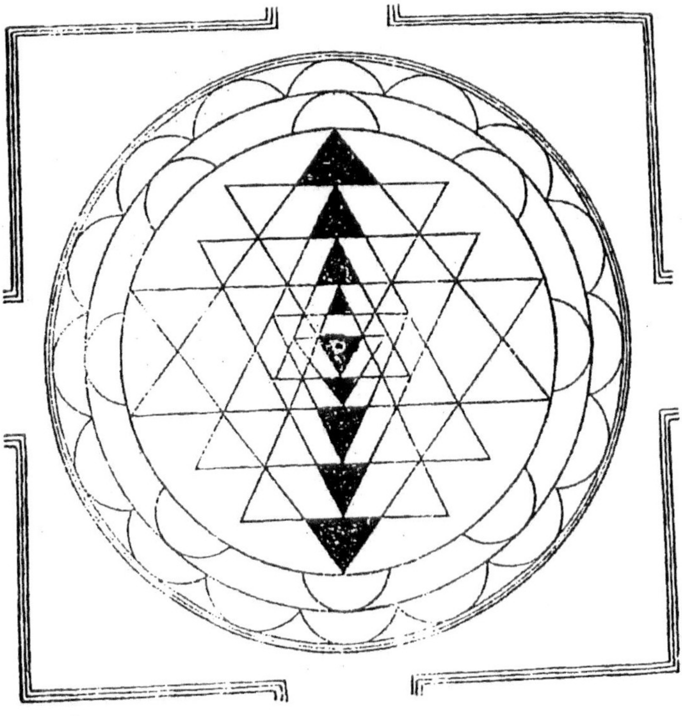

चतुर्भिः शविचक्रैश्च पञ्चभिः।
शिवशक्तयात्मकं ज्ञेयं श्रीचक्रं शिवयोर्वपुः॥

Introduction

YANTRA, MANTRA AND TANTRA

उपास्यायाः परमेश्वर्यायाः त्रीणि रूपाणि उपास्तियोग्यनिस्थूलं सूक्ष्मं परं चेति। तत्राद्यं करचरणाद्यवयवशीलं...., द्वितीयं मन्त्रात्मकं, श्रवणेंन्द्रियवागिन्द्रिययोग्यं..., तृतीय वासनात्मकं मनसो योग्यं...॥

Religious devotion assumes three modes, sometimes alternate but often complementary :

1. It conceives the object of religious devotion (*viz.*, God) in a familiar human form, albeit with modifications suited to religious imagination and mystic idiom. It appeals to people who are extroverts, whose intellectual equipment is modest, and whose religious commitment compromises worldly attractions and involvements. The Godhead becomes meaningful to them only when represented as an icon (*mūrti*) with familiar details, although they do recognize that the icon is merely symbolic and stylized in the context of cultural realities.

2. The second mode is relevant to the religious devotion of people who are extroverts as well as introverts as occasion demands or necessitates, whose intellectual equipment is of a higher order

than those of the above group, and whose religious commitment is deeper and can withstand worldly attractions and involvements. They imagine the Godhead as consisting of primordial verbal modalities (*mantra*), *viz.*, the source of all transactions and relations in the human context, and essential ingredients of all self-expression and communication.

3. The third mode is applicable to people whose constitution is more refined and evolved than that of the two former classes. They are mostly introverts, and their religious commitment is deep, firm and intense. Worldly attractions and involvements are for them feeble. They visualize Godhead as beyond both physical form and verbal modality, but as transcendental although unfailing source of all thoughts and feelings.

The three modes correspond to the three-fold nature of man : body, speech and mind. The first mode of religious devotion needs a concrete physical representation of the object of devotion, for the expression of devotion must involve bodily actions suggestive of a worshipful attitude. Worship accompanied by elaborate rituals, pilgrimages, ceremonials, monumental and artistic representation of divinities are illustrations of this mode. The second mode dispenses with such crude physical props, and relies upon man's capacity to intensely articulate his thoughts and feelings in the sounds of speech, pregnant with symbol and meaning. The approach to Godhead here is principally through prayers, magical formulae and other similar devices to express the inexpressible. It is usual for these verbal formulation to become culturally specific and traditionally stylized. The third mode seeks to go beyond both body and speech, and utilize the powers of man's mind to reflect, cogitate, explore, understand and concentrate. The approach here is independent of the familiar modes of perception, transaction and communication.

The first mode of religious devotion has a strong social base; the individual learns and assimilates the mores and modalities current in the group to which he belongs, and seldom feels the need to challenge them or ignore them. Religious devotion expresses itself in group activities, in forms of behaviour that are specific to communities. The second mode also functions in a group context, but the individual, although physically involved in the group, is in effect an isolate. His prayers and abracadabra are no doubt learnt from the group and shared by the group-members; but they are articulated with an emphasis on his own experiences and expectations. The third mode, however, is entirely individualistic. There is no physical activity or verbal behaviour that the individual devotee shares with others. Thoughts are his own, strictly private and relevant to his own intellectual and intuitive development. Of course, even they are culturally stylized and transmitted through generations. But this mode manifests itself in the meditative isolation of the individual.

Religion in India has explored the possibilities of all three of these modes which may roughly be described as iconic worship, prayer, and meditation. Godhead is represented in a myriad forms, familiar and unfamiliar, charming and grotesque, simple and complex, crude and artistic, for use at home and in public places. Rituals have also been structured and stylized. Religious literature, at once vast and varied, has also taken shape, crystallizing prayers and magical formulations in all the languages current in the country, but mainly in Sanskrit. Ideational exercises too have been practised and prescribed, as part of religious devotion in all the religious denominations prevalent in the country.

The three modes coexist not only peacefully but also to mutual advantage, in India. We often find the same individual indulging in all three modes, without being in the least embarrassed by the paradox this may suggest. Sometimes, the three modes are taken up in a graded sequence : starting with physical and ritualistic worship, going to intense verbal articulations and closing by meditational sessions.

The three modes are known in India by the expressions: *yantra, mantra,* and *tantra.* The Sanskrit word *yantra* strictly means a contrivance, device, or gadget; a mechanism to serve a purpose; and something of instrumental value. In the religious context, it means physical representations of the objects of worship, iconic images (*pratimā*) in a human, quasi-human or animal form; aniconic objects, either natural (like the black ammonite stone found in the Gaṇḍakī river (*śālagrāma*) or round pebble got from the Narmadā river (*bāṇa-liṅga*), or crystal (*maṇi*), or artifacts like the *liṅgas*, or weapons like the discuss of Vishṇu, trident of Śiva, or the spear of Devī); or symbolic diagrams (*maṇḍala*), either linear or three-dimensional. Icons are regarded as concrete (or manifest, *vyakta*) representations of divinity, while aniconic objects are both concrete and abstract (*vyaktāvyakta*), and symbolic diagrams altogether abstract (*avyakta*).

The word *mantra* signified "thought that protects' (*mananāt trāṇanāt*); thoughts that are crystallized into powerful words or syllables, intense brooding over which (or sustained repetition of which) is expected to protect the person from hearts and afflictions. The *mantras* are manifold in accordance with the forms of the divinity; but they are all alike representations of the divinity in stylized verbal forms. The *mantras* are not only modes of contact with the divinity, but are themselves divinities. They are, therefore, held in great reverence, and communicated only to eligible persons and in reverent solemnity. They are of three kinds in their articulation: clearly and audibly articulated (*vāchika*); muttered inaudibly but with movement of lips (*upāṁśu*); and only mentally formed (*mānasa*). The last is regarded as the most effectual, the first least and the second moderately so.

There are correspondences between *yantra* and *mantra*. When worship is conducted and rituals gone through, prayers and incantations are invariably uttered. The object of worship is as much represented in the *yantra* as in the *mantra*. If *yantra* is a visual representation of divinity, mantra is the thought-word symbol of it. The two together constitute a whole and either without the other is ineffectual and incomplete.

Tantra is the extension of thought processes into the mysterious realms of divinity, riding over both visual representations and verbal formulations. It is integrative in its function; it seeks to actualize the object of religious devotion by synthesizing the *yantra* and the *mantra* aspects of the divinity. While it makes use of rituals as well as prayers and incantations, its main approach is to realign the individual's energies to harmonize with the cosmic energies. It draws out the forces hidden in the human constitution, muffled by worldly involvements and constricted by the physical factors; it also facilitates extra-individual forces descend into the human constitution.

The word *tantra* etymologically signifies 'spread' or 'extension' (*tan- 'vistāra'*) and 'protection by explanation' (*tattri-dhāraṇa*). They not only extend the energies, but preserve them by elaborate rituals and verbal explanations. The *tantra* actually refers to a group of texts, which attempt to explain the normally inexplicable, to clarify the mysteries and to prescribe procedures by means of which the reorganization of human energy may take place. These texts also project a comprehensive point of view, a philosophy of religious devotion that takes into account the factors of normal human constitution as well as the essential realities of the universe.

Chapter 1

The Yantra of Srī-Chakra

1. The Composition of Śrī-Chakra

The employment of *yantras* for worship is widespread. Even when icon are used, it is usual to inscribe stylized and appropriate geometrical designs in from of the icon (if it is stationary) and conduct the worship rituals on them; if the icon is mobile, it is placed right on the inscribed design and worshipped. The design signifies consecrated ground, or site on which spiritual forces are gathered. The preparation of the design involves the transformation of an ordinary ground into an effective ground, the inert idol into a powerful icon, and the normal mind of the devotee into an efficient instrument for the rituals. It is not the icon that transmits this power to the design; in fact, the icon derives its merit by its involvement in the design. It is the intentionality of the devotee, along with the traditionally transmitted pattern that makes the design a powerful facility.

It is technically known as *maṇḍala*, 'that which gathers the essential details' (*maṇḍam lāti*). *Tantra-rāja-tantra* describes the nature and uses of *maṇḍala* in worship as well as meditation. *Maṇḍala* is the concentration of the most significant aspect of the world in which the devotee lives and seeks to carry out his devotion; it is the concentration of the most significant aspects of the devotee's own constitution for the purpose of the devotions, and it is also the concentration of the most significant aspect of the interaction between the devotee and his world. It is a vehicle of concentration, so that all the relevant details are centered. Maṇḍala in this sense is defined as a collection of energies (*śakti-samūha*) and as a symbol (*saṅketa*).

'Center' (*bindu*) is in fact the origin of the *maṇḍala.* The diffuse, and therefore feeble, forces are gathered up from all the sides, rendering them powerful by the very act of gathering up. They are made to converge into the center of the *maṇḍala,* which is identical with the center of the devotee's own being. The forces of the universe are concentrated in the *maṇḍala*, and at the same time, the energies of the psychophysical constitution of the devotee is also centered in the same *maṇḍala.* This idea is conveyed by the Sanskrit expression 'samhāra' or 'samhṛti' (dissolution, absorption).

The other process involved in the *maṇḍala* is the potential extension of the essential details on all sides from the center. The center is the seed from which the tree of spiritual transaction sprouts and spreads alround. Forces of transformation, integration and harmony that lie dormant in the center of the *maṇḍala* emanate on all sides and fill the devotee and the world in which the lives. This function of the *maṇḍala* is called 'sṛshṭi' (projection, creation, emanation).

The *maṇḍala* thus is meant to activate the energies both within the devotee and outside him. It is a psycho-cosmic mechanism for effectively relating the inner space (*viz.*, the space of individualized consciousness, *chittākāśa*) with the outer space (*viz.*, the three-dimensional world, *mahākāśa*) in the comprehensive space of essential consciousness which rejects the subject-object dichotomy altogether (*chidākāśa*). The world is a mechanism for objectification of consciousness (*prameya*) while the individual is a mechanism for subjectification of consciousness (*pramātā*). In the conflicting directions of the two modes, stress is unavoidable. The purpose of the *maṇḍala* is to eliminate this stress by harmonizing the two modes.

The significance of the midmost point or center of the *maṇḍala* is its utter freedom from dimensions. The Sanskrit word 'bindu' also means 'seed,' 'sperm', 'drop' : it not only concentrates but becomes the dynamic starting-point. In gathers up the outside forces into a point, and beings to unfold the inner forces. It also represents the point at which the outer space and the inner space meet and have their rest.

Thus the *maṇḍala* is a psychocosmogram; a plan of the presented universe and of the perceiving individual. The entire universe is stylized into a pattern of energies that is symbolized by the layout of the *maṇḍala*. The reorganization of the individual in terms of the same *maṇḍala* makes the *maṇḍala* an effective model for transformation, projection, concentration and integration. Consciousness of the individuals finds its articulation and expansion in the model thus provided.

The *maṇḍala* is in its nature a complex pattern of several geometrical patterns, each of which has a specific character and a special function. Tradition has standardized the import of several patterns like the triangle with its apex on top (masculine energy), the triangle with its apex at the bottom (feminine energy), circle (cyclical dynamism of conscious- ness), square (the physical world made up of the elements), and circle of lotus petals (regeneration of powers and principles).

The principle of the *maṇḍala* drawing is to represent the universe as an enclosed field for the play of consciousness. There would usually be a series of enclosures, facilitating movement inwards and outwards; and the whole figure would be surrounded by an outer band of square or circle (or 'belt of fire', *Me-Ri* in the Tibetan *maṇḍala*), with gateways facing the cardinal points. The entire *maṇḍala* is viewed as a city (*pura*), a palace (*prāsāda*) or an island (*dvipa*). The midmost point or area is considered the residence of the great one who presides over the city, who rules in the palace, or rests in the island. When the *maṇḍala* is made to represent the human constitution itself, areas of the *maṇḍala* are made to correspond with the parts of the body, and the projected body-*maṇḍala* is presided over by the 'self' in the inmost sanctum. Introspective visualization helps in giving meaning to the *maṇḍala*.

The *maṇḍala* is frequently a representation of the mythical mountain Meru, made of solid gold (*hemādri*) and studded with jewels (*ratnasānu*), the resplendent abode of the gods. The mountain is also the highest peak in the world, located in the very center of the universe, illumining the four quarters by its lustre.[1] In fact, our temples and stūpas are architectural efforts to reproduce the imagery of mount Meru. It may be remembered that the tāntrik ideology is intimately related to the culture of mountain; and mountains are especially sacred to the mother-goddesses for whom the mountain peaks, difficult to ascend, are fortresses (*durga*). The human body is also a Meru, with its highest peak in the thousand-petalled lotus (*sahasrāra*) where the Self resides. In keeping with the idea of a fortress, the *maṇḍala* would have ramparts (*prākāra*), entrances (*dvāra*), guards (*dvāra-pāla*), lines of defence (*ara* or *aśra*), areas of succor (*dala*), corners (*koṇa*), arches (*toraṇa*), garlands (*hāra*) and courtyards (*aṅgaṇa*). In the Mahāyāna texts dealing with *maṇḍala*, 'maṇḍa' is made to mean 'what is contained', defended or 'held', and *la* to mean 'that which contains', 'defends' or 'holds'.[2]

The rituals pertaining to the mandala, which activate the hidden forces both within the external diagram and in the devotee's constitution, involve the proper positioning of the tutellary deities (*kula-devatā*), captains (*nāyikā*), aids (*yoginī*) and guards (*mudrā-devatā*). Their locations are determined according to the tāntrik prescriptions, and the purpose for which the *maṇḍala* is used. The placement of the retinue divinities is sometimes accomplished by inscribing appropriate letters of the alphabet in different areas of the *maṇḍala*. The Sanskrit alphabet is regarded as the vocal epitome of the entire universe, and each letter is transformed into an energy when introduced into the *maṇḍala*.

बिन्दु-त्रिकोण-वसुकोण-दशारयुग्म-
मन्वश्र-नागदलसंयुत-षोडशारं।
वृत्तत्रयं च धरणीसदनत्रयं च
श्रीचक्रमेतदुदितं परदेवतरायाः।।

Śrī-chakra is a *maṇḍala* which is regarded as the body of the mother goddess known variously as Devī, Tripurā-Sundarī, Lalitā, Rāja-rājeśvarī, and Parā-bhaṭṭārikā. The design also represents this divinity's court, with all the attendant-deities, aids, guards, pavilions, enclosures and entrances. The principal divinity (*viz.*, the mother-goddess) is imagined as being seated in the central point (*bindu*) on a cot, the four legs of which are the deities responsible for creation of all things (Brahmā) in North-East, preservation (Vishṇu) in the South-East, dissolution (rudra) in South-West, and withdrawal (Īśāna) in North-West; and the plank of which is the principle of acceptance and retention of the withdrawn world until recreation, also signifying the divinity's favour (*anugraha*), symbolized as Sadāśiva. These five principles are described as the five activities of the mother-goddess; they are her five modes of expression.[3] There is also an explanation that these five represent the five inert dimensions, 'ghostlike' (*pañcha-preta*), which are enlivened by the mother-goddess seated on them, four of them serving as the legs of the cot and the fifth being the plank. She is the life-giver; without her, even the god Śiva is like unto a corpse (*śava*). It is only when inspired by her that he is able to bring forth the manifold universe; bereft of her inspiration he is unable even to move. When conjoined with her, he becomes Kāmeśvara, the effective master of desire.

The central point (*bindu*) is thus a union of the ultimate male principle (*purusha*) and the ultimate female principle (*prakṛti*); the former is the principle of consciousness (Śiva) while the latter is energy (Śakti). The symbolism permeates the whole composition of Śrī-chakra, which is described as 'body of Śiva and Śivā' (the passive male and the active Female)[4] The Male is symbolized in the triangle with its apex upwards (*viz.*, away from us when held horizontally in front of us), and the Female is symbolized by the triangle with its apex downwards, (*viz.*, towards us). The former is known as the 'Male field' (*Śiva-chakra*) and the latter 'Female field' (*śakti-chakra*).

Śrī-chakra is essentially a pattern of interwoven triangles, nine in number, four of which represent the male principles (*śiva-chakra*), identified with Brahma, Rudra, Īśvara, and Sadāśiva and five female principles (*śakti-chakra*) identified with *Śrī-vidyā*, Tvaritā, Pārijāteśvari, Tripurā and Pañchabāṇeśi.[5] The chakra is therefore called *nava-yonyāt-maka-chakra, viz.*, the pattern which constitutes nine-fold union. The numbers three and nine are significant in Śrī-chakra.[6] The triangle has three angles (*tri-koṇa*), hence the deity which it represents is called *'Tri-putā'* ('one that has three fields'). The symbolism will be explained later. But it must be mentioned here that the triangle itself is an emanation from, or a projection of, the central point (*bindu*), which is itself an unmanifest union of Śiva and Śakti (see the section on Tantra). And there are nine triangles in all, four representing Śiva and five Śakti, the commingling of which illustrates the same union but in a manifest manner. The nine triangles interwoven project as many as forty-four triangles, if we count the central point (*bindu*) also as a triangle, as is usually done. Sometimes, however, the midmost point is excluded, for it does not have the manifest form of a triangle, and then the number of triangles would be forty-three.

This pattern of forty-four triangles (or forty-three formal triangles together with the central point *bindu*) constitutes the main design of Śrī-chakra. Surrounding this pattern, however, are two concentric circles (called lotuses), inner one having eight petals (*dala*) and the outer sixteen. These in turn are enclosed by three concentric circles (called 'girdles', *valaya*). And the whole design is placed inside a square field (called courtyard or 'earth-stretch' *bhūpura*), in the form of three lines signifying enclosures. On each side of the square is a portal or gateway (*dvāra*).

This, then, is the composition of the Śrī-chakra : three-angled figures (*tri-koṇa*) arranged in nine successive coverings or enclosures (*navāvaraṇa*). The nine enclosures from the interior to the exterior are enumerated formally thus :

1. the central point (*bindu*) which is regarded as *Śiva-chakra;*
2. the primary triangle (*tri-koṇa*);
3. a figure with eight corners also consisting of eight smaller triangles surrounding the primary triangle (*ashṭa-koṇa*, also called *vasu-koṇa*);
4. a figure with ten angles (also ten triangles), surrounding the above (*daśa-koṇa* or *daśāra*);
5. an other figure of ten angles (also ten triangles), surrounding the above (and therefore called *bahir-daśāra,* outer ten-angled figure, in contradistinction with the above, which is called, in relation to this, *antar-daśāra* 'inner ten-angled figure);

6. a figure with fourteen angles (also triangles) surrounding the above (*chatur-daśāra*); these five (from 2 to 6) being regarded as 'Female-fields' (*śakti-chakras*);
7. a circle in the form of a lotus with eight petals (*ashṭa-dala-padma*) enclosing the above main part of Śrī-chakra;
8. another circle surrounding the above in the form of a lotus with sixteen petals (*shoḍaśa-patraka*) and
9. the square field in which the above is positioned (*chaturaśra* or *bhūpura*); these three together with the first, *viz.*, the central point, being the four 'Male fields' (*śiva-chakras*).

Not included in the main pattern but figuring in the composition of Śrī-chakra are the three concentric circles (*tri-valaya* or *tri-vṛtta*) representing the triple worlds, surrounding the 8th of the enclosures (*viz.*, *shoḍaśa-patraka*) and the three lines (*tri-rekhā*) surrounding the 9th enclosure (*viz.*, *bhūpura*).

While the usual view[7] is that among the nine triangles that constitute the main portion of Śrī-chakra, four represent Śiva and five Śakti, there is also a view[8] that all the nine triangles are śakti-chakras, representing nine female deities (or aspects of the mother goddess) : Vāmā, Jyeshṭhā, Raudrī, Aṁbikā, Parāśakti (represented by the so-called 'female' triangles), Icchā, Jnanā, Kriyā and Śāntā (represented by the four so-called 'male' triangles).

In the main design of Śrī-chakra, composed of the nine commingling triangles, the angles are of course of primary importance. They signify the points of union of Śiva and Śakti; and they are so many projections of the central point (*bindu*) which is enclosed by the fundamental triangle (known as *Kāma-kalā*), signifying the residence of the mother-goddess. Besides these angles, there are two other kinds of points in the main design that are held sacred; the points where two lines unite (or intersect) (*sandhi,* defined as 'dvi-rekhā-saṅgama-sthānam') and the points where three lines meet (*marma-sthāna* or vital points, defined as 'tri-rekhā-saṅgama-sthānam'). There are twenty-four unions and twenty eight meeting points in the design, There are of course no such angles, unions or meeting points outside the main design, enclosed by the three concentric circles (*tri-vṛtta*).

The motif of the union of Śiva and Śakti is sought to be evoked in the entire Śrī-chakra in a more comprehensive way. The various geometrical forms that are involved are seen as pairing off:[9] the central point (*bindu*) with the fundamental triangle (*tri-koṇa*); the eight-cornered figure inside (*ashṭāra*) with the eight-petalled lotus (*ashṭa-dala-padma*) outside; the two ten-angled figures (*daśāra*, the inner and the outer) inside the girdle with the 16-petalled lotus (*shodaśa-patraka*) outside; and the 14-petalled figure (*chatur-daśāra*) with the surrounding square (*chaturaśra, bhūpura*).

The union of Śiva and Śakti is the central idea in Śrī-chakra; it is in fact the corner-stone of the *Śrī-vidyā* philosophy. If the universe is comprehended by the twenty-five psycho-physical principles (*tattva*) which are fundamental to existence and experience, in accordance with the systemic framework provided to all Indian thought by the Sāṁkhya school, the commingling of Śiva and Śakti (*śiva-śakti-yoga*) is the twenty-sixth principle (*tattva*), which pervades the whole design but in an unmanifest manner.

The nine chakras represent the initial emanation of the phenomenal universe from this transcendental principle (*sṛshṭi*), intermediary preservation of the order, growth and harmony in the universe (*sthiti*), and the ultimate dissolution (*viz.*, not destruction but absorption) of the universe (*saṁ-hāra*). The there chakras that are on the periphery (*viz.*, the square *bhūpura*, sixteen-petalled lotus and the eight-petalled lotus) are known together as the centre of emanation (*sṛshṭi-chakra*). The two chakras that constitute the middle portion (*viz.*, fourteen-cornered figure and the two ten-angled figures, inner and outer) are known as the centre of preservation (*sthiti-chakra*); and the three interior chakras (*viz.*, eight-angled figure, the primary triangle and the central point) are known as the centre of absorption (*samhāra-chakra*). The first center is said to be presided over by Moon (*soma*), the second by Sun (*sūrya*) and the third by Fire (*agni*). The significance of the triad (*tripura*) will be explained in the section on the Tantra of Śrī-chakra.

2. Preparation of Śrī-Chakra

There are two ways of counting the nine enclosures : one, starting from the central point (*bindu*) and going outwards, ending with the square that surrounds the whole design (*bhūpura*); and the other, starting with the outermost square and proceeding inwards till the central point is reached. These methods are in accordance with the two traditions of preparing the Śrī-chakra and also conducting worship.

The 'Kaula' method of preparing the Śrī-chakra follows the method of 'absorption' (*saṁhāra-krama*), and is given in Lakshmīdhara's commentary on *Saundarya-laharī*, verse 11 :

1. A circle is drawn first; and within it nine paralled and equidistant, lines are drawn across, beginning with the bottom-most and going up, three short lines occupying the central portion, on either side of which a line touches the circle on both sides; and beyond these lines are two other lines of decreasing length. These nine lines serve as bases for the nine triangles that constitute the Śrī-chakra. These lines are said to represent the nine stellar bodies : sun, moon, *aṅgāraka, budha, bṛhaspati, śukra, śani, rāhu* and *ketu.* The first four represent the Śiva factor, while the latter five the Śakti factor.

2. Then, lines are drawn from the ends of the topmost line, making them converge in the centre of the sixth line below, thus forming the first triangle (with apex downwards).

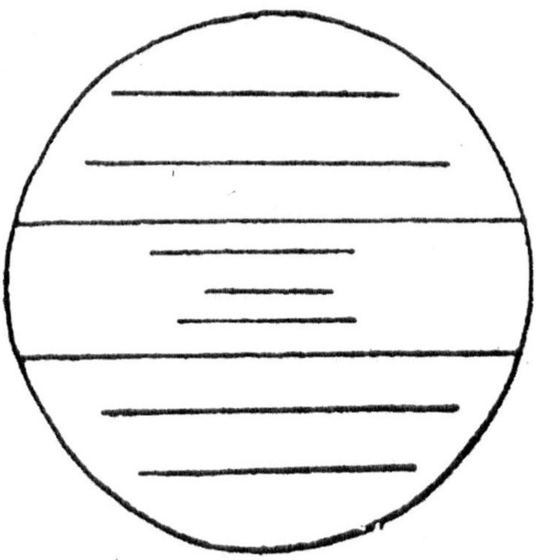

Another triangle (with apex upwards) is similarly formed by converging the lines drawn from the ends of the bottom-most line in the centre of the seventh line above. The two triangles will intersect, and in the process, is formed the primary triangle within which the central point is inserted.

Then, from the ends of the second top line are drawn two lines that converge in the centre of the eight line below.

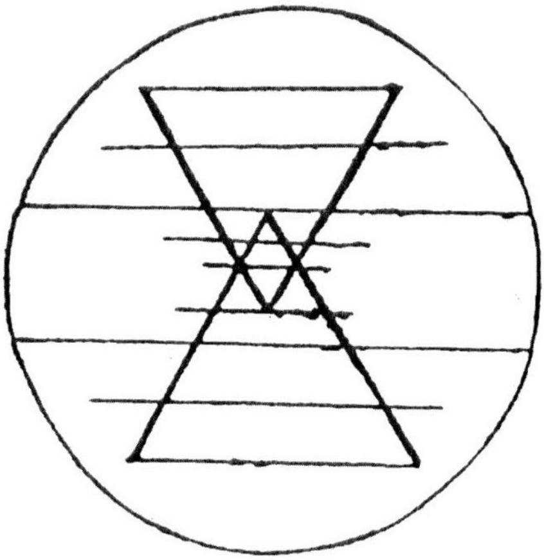

3. The lines from the ends of the second line (from top) are drawn and made to converge in the centre of the ninth line (bottom-most), and likewise the lines drawn thus forming another set of two interesting triangles.

4. The two long lines that run across and touch the sides of the circle are then taken up. Lines from the ends of these lines are drawn so as to form a triangle, the apex of

which touches the circle. The two intersecting triangles thus formed produce a six-angled figure (*shaṭ-koṇa*).

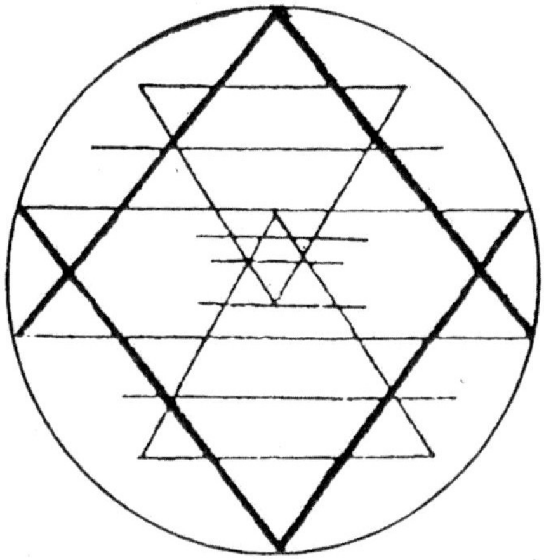

5. Two of the three lines in the middle portion of the circle are now taken up. The ends of the line on top are drawn so as to converge at the centre of the fifth line (counted

from this top line) below, and similarly the ends of the line at the bottom are drawn so as to converge at the centre of the fifth line above (counted from this bottom line). Thus, two intersecting triangles are got.

6. The shortest of the three lines in the middle portion, which is also the midmost line among the nine lines, is finally taken up. The lines from the two ends of it are made to converge in the centre of the third line from it.

The 'Samaya' method of preparing the Śrī-chakra, following the method of 'emanation' (*sṛshti*), is given in *Jñānārṇava-tantra* (cf. also *Śrī-vidyārṇava-tantra,* 1, 8, 10-33). It begins by drawing a triangle (inside which is the *bindu*) with its apex upwards (*viz.,* facing west, or away from the devotee), and by drawing another triangle with apex downwards (or towards the devotee), cutting the first triangle above the *bindu.* A third triangle formed, apex upwards, from a base drawn across the apex of the first triangle. Thus is formed the pattern of eight triangles (*ashṭ a-koṇa*), and on this basis the pattern of ten inner triangles (*antar-daśāra*), the pattern of ten outer triangles (*bahir-daśāra*) and the pattern of fourteen triangles (*chaturdaśāra*) are drawn. Successive extension of the lines is the main procedure employed here; and the principles involved are increasing the number of triangles from one to three, from three to eight, and from eight to ten, and distinguishing of the meeting places of lines (*sandhi* and *marma*), thereby forming fourteen triangles out of the outer ten.

Thus, there will be nine triangles, four of them with apex upwards (*viz.*, away from the devotee), signifying the fields of Śiva or Agni, and five with apex downwards (*viz.*, towards the devotee) signifying the Śakti-fields, 43 angles, 24 *sandhis* (points where two lines intersect) and 24 (or 28 according to Lakshmīdhara) *marmas* (where three lines meet).

The main differences between the two methods are with regard to the posture of the primary triangle and the position of the central point (*bindu*). In the Kaula method, the primary triangle faces downwards (*viz.*, forming the field of Śakti) and the *bindu* is located in its midmost area. In the Samaya method, however, the primary triangle faces upwards (*viz.*, forming the field of Śiva or Agni) and the *bindu* is located in the midmost point of the area enclosed by the six-angled figure (including the primary triangle). The Kaula method disregards the number of angles; it holds as relevant only the *marma-sthānas* (points where three lines meet) formed by the nine triangles.

Drawing the eight-petalled lotus and the sixteen-petalled lotus surrounding this main portion, encircling the whole by three lines on all sides are done at the end, alike in both methods. In fact, they are regarded as inessential details, and are even altogether dispensed with in some traditions (as for instance in the Hayagrīva-saṁpradāya), while in some other traditions they are drawn as decorative details and are not involved in the worship rituals (as in the Ānanda-bhairava-saṁpradāya). It is only in the tradition known after Dakshiṇāmūrti that these peripheral details are held as important as the interior pattern of nine triangles.

There are two varieties of the *yantra* with regard to Śrī-chakra. The first, and the most commonly found, variety is the linear *yantra*, Śrī-chakra is drawn with a stylus using sandal paste, turmeric, *kuṁkum, gorochana,* or coloured ink as medium on a specially prepared ground, on a wooden plank, or on the flattened bark of some approved tree, on *bhūrja* or palm-leaf, or on paper. It may alternately be inscribed on a metal sheet, gold, silver or copper, in order of preference. The potency of the *yantra* in gold is said to endure for a life-time, of the *yantra* in silver for thirty-two years, and of the *yantra* in copper for twelve years (*Ratnasāgara*). The golden *yantra* is said to promote worldly influence, the silver one health and long life, the copper one wealth; and the one made in all three metals together is said to secure all accomplishments. The metals that are unsuited for this purpose are iron, lead and zinc. Crystals are recommended as excellent material for inscribing the *yantra*. It should, however, never be written or hung on a wall, a screen or a pillar. Worship must always be conducted to the Śrī-chakra kept in a horizontal position, with the apex of the primary triangle facing the devotee.

The other variety is three-dimensional. This is called *meru,* because it assumes the form of a mountain. If the form is that of a low mountain, it is *ardha-meru.* It may be carved in stone or crystal, cut in precious and semi-precious stones, or cast in metal (gold, silver, or copper as mentioned above). Unlike the linear variety where all the nine chakras are on the same plane, this variety projects the chakras on different elevations. There are three sub-varieties in the latter: (*a*) the three outer chakras (*viz., sṛshṭi-chakra*) all on the bottom level, the three middle chakras (*shiti-chakra*) on the middle level, and the three inner chakras (*saṁhāra-chakra*) on the top level; (*b*) the outer square (*bhūpura*) on the bottom level, the lotus of sixteen petals (*shoḍaśāra*) and the lotus of eight petals (*ashṭa-dala padma*) on the middle level, and the main portion (*viz.*, the nine triangles intersecting) all on the top level (inscribed or embossed on a flat surface; and (*c*) each of the nine chakras is on a different elevation, and the *meru* looks like a gradually rising mountain peak, with the square base (*bhūpura*) and pointed top (*bindu*), other chakras being arranged in the ascending order.

The layout of Śrī-chakra is three-fold. Where emanation of the phenomenal universe from the central point (*sṛshṭi*) is the prevailing idea, the chakras are arranged in the form of a mountain and are identified with the sixteen *nityā* deities (see section on the Tantra of Śrī-chakra). The layout then is called *meru-prastāra;* it is prescribed as suitable for celibates and the less evolved devotees. When the prevailing idea is

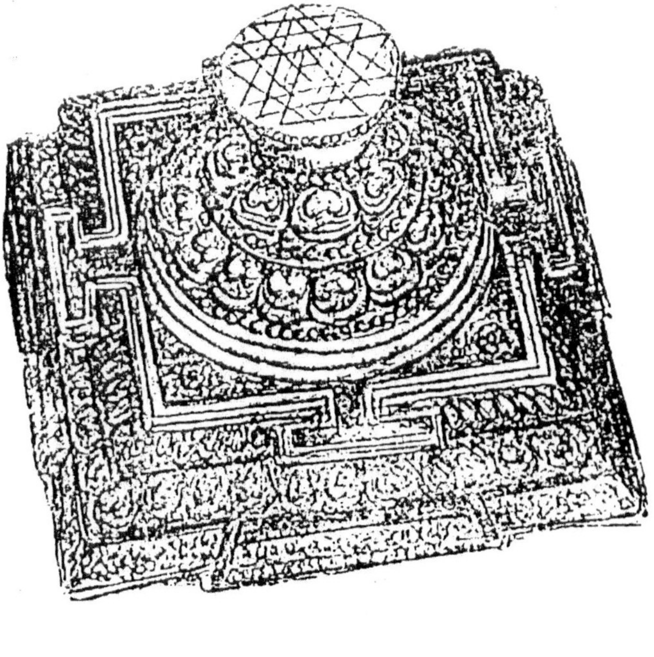

preservation of the universe (*sthiti*), the chakras are all laid out on the same plane and are identified with vaśini-vagdevatas (see section on the Tantra). The layout in this case is called *bhū-prastāra;* and is recommended as suitable for householders. When, however, the idea of disolution (*laya*) prevails, the central point (*bindu*) stands out prominently, and the other chakras are arranged in one, two, or three elevations, and are identified with the *mātṛkās* (see section on the Tantra). The layout here is called *Kailāsa-prastāra,* recommended for ascetics and renunciants.[10]

There is another way of classifying the Śrī-chakras, which is simpler than the above. When the entire design is inscribed, embossed, or drawn on a flat surface in flush with the ground, it is called *bhū-pṛshṭha.* When the inscribed, embossed, or drawn design is supported by a dwarf pedestal, raised like the back of a tortoise, it is called *kacchapa-pṛshṭ ha.* When the inscribed, embossed, or drawn design is held aloft by a tall structure, or when the design assumes the form of a mountain with the chakras on different elevations, it is called *meru-pṛshṭha.*

Further, the *yantras* of *Śrī*-chakra fall into three groups according to the modes of their employment. When the *yantra* is a permanent one (inscribed on stone or on metal plates, or carved in stone, or cast in metals), and fixed to the ground, it is *achara* ('immovable'). Once it is ceremonially installed and consecrated, it becomes worthy of worship for all time, without any need for periodical renewals. If, on the other hand, the *yantra* is drawn by hand on an earthern plate, on a wooden plank, on *bhūrja* surface or on paper, or inscribed on a metal plate not fixed to a pedestal, its efficacy depends upon its proper consecration before the worship rituals begin; and it ceases to be worthy of repeated worship when once it is used. On each occasion of worship, the *yantra* must be prepared anew and consecrated afresh. Not being fixed to the ground, such a *yantra* could be carried about, and thus it is called *chara* ('mobile'). The third group of *yantras* consists of the design inscribed or carved in metal, crystal, gem and so on and own on the body (as pendants, rings or amulets). These are necessarily small in size, and do not admit of ritualistic worship. They are, therefore, not consecrated in any manner. This group is called *dhāraṇa-yogya*. Its efficacy consists in its being touched and given by a holy man; it has no value when bought in a market.

3. The Nine Enclosures

Śrī-chakra is visualized as an elaborate mansion, in the innermost apartment of which abides the mother-goddess in all her majesty and glory. But the mansion presents a series of coverings or enclosures, passing through which we reach the sanctum. Each of these coverings hides the divine presence in a series of phenomenal and psychical projections and presentations; but it is suffused by the divine presence. It can also illumine the devotees's path. That is why each of these enclosures (*āvaraṇa*) is regarded as a step to further our journey towards the sanctum of the mother-goddess, as a station in our onward spiritual progress.

There are nine of these coverings or enclosures (*āvara-ṇa* from root *vṛ*, 'to cover'), beginning with the surrounding square, significantly called 'the earth-stretch' (*bhū-pura*), and ending with the central point (*bindu*), which is the natural abode of the mother-goddess. Each of these has its own name, physical form and spiritual significance; its own appropriate colour (signifying the approach tendencies), a presiding divinity (*chakranāyikā* or *chakreśvarī*) who is merely a variant form of the mother goddess abiding in the central point, a class of specific aids in the spiritual progress (*yoginī*) representing different aspects of the mother-goddess, and a particular guard-divinity (*mudrā-debatā*) who welcomes, purifies and delights the devotee (*mudam rāti*). The spiritual aids are 64 crores in number, and they constitute the retinue of the mother-goddess (*mahāchatuh-shashṭi-yoginī-gaṇa-sevitā*).

Thus, Śrī-chakra is verily the body of the mother-goddess, her own form.[11] The nine enclosures actually reveal her true form to the devotee and hence worship of each of these is enjoined on the devotee. The worship rituals involve the presiding deities, aids and guards mentioned above. The worship sequence begins with the outer-most enclosure (*bhūpura*) and is completed at the innermost enclosure (*viz.*, the central point, *bindu*).

1. *First Enclosure,* called 'Deluder of the three realms' (*Trailokyamohana*).

The form is that of an 'all-inclusive square' (*sarvānta-chaturaśra*). It is the wide space in which the entire *yantra* is poised. On its outer fringe are three lines (*tri-rekhā*), like ramparts of a fortress (*prākāra*), one inside the other, and coloured, white, red and yellow, in order. On the inner edge of the space are three concentric circle (*tri-vṛtta*) surrounding the sixteen-petalled lotus.

The square provides a gateway (portal) on each side called *āmnāya* (East, South, West and North). The outer-most line surrounding this square is the residence of the then spirits of spiritual accomplishment (*siddhis*), four of them stationed at the four portals, another four at the four

corners, one above and one below. These spirits represent abilities to become minute (*aṇimā*), swell into magnitude (*mahimā*), become light (*laghimā*), become heavy (*garimā*), to lord over (*īśitva*), to desire (*icchā*), to subjugate (*vaśitva*), to attain the objects of desire (*prākāmya*), to get pleasures (*bhukti*), and to actualize all intentions (*sarva-kāma-siddhi*), These are powers to be acquired for self-protection along the spiritual journey.

The second line surrounding the square represents the eight minor 'mother deities' (*mātṛkas*), four of them stationed at the doors and four at the corners. They are creatures of passionate longing (*Brāhmī*), of violent anger (*Māheśvarī*) of insatiable avarice (*Kaumārī*), of dazed fascination for the world (*Vaishṇavī*), of piggish obstinacy (*Vārāhī*), of tormenting jealousy (*Indrāṇī*), of sinful disturbances (*Chāmuṇḍā*) and of benign inspiration towards merit (*Mahālakshmī*). They have their consorts (*bhairavas*) : black-bodied Asitāṅga, indignant Ruru, fierce Chaṇḍa, thoughtless Krodha, intoxicated and ground Unmatta, envious Kapāla, terrible Bhīshaṇa, and absorbing Saṁhāra respectively.

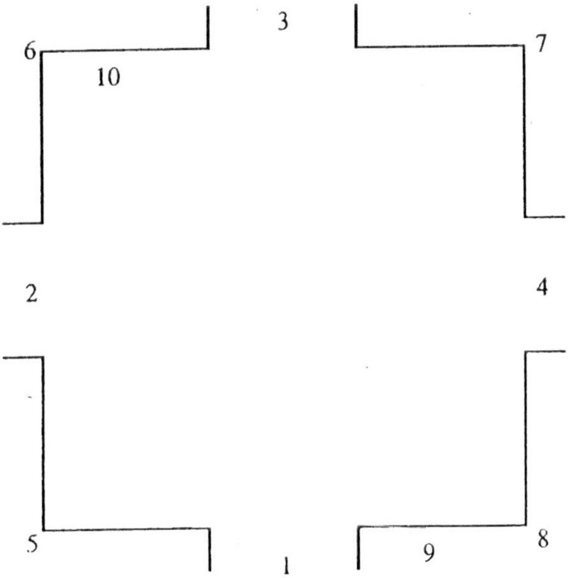

The inner line surrounding the square represents ten feminine guards (*mudrā-śakti*) or guardians of the ten directions (*dikpālas*) : Sarvasaṁkshobhiṇī ('agitating all') stationed in the West; Sarvavidrāviṇī ('chasing all') in the North, Sarvākarshiṇī ('fascinating all') in the East, Sarvavaśaṁ-karī (subjugating all') in the South, Sarvonmādiṇī ('driving all mad') in North-West, Sarvāṅkuśā ('goading all') in North-East, Khecharī ('moving about in thin air') in South-East, Sarvabīkjā ('sprouting everything') in South-West, Mahā-yoni ('the great source of all things') below, and Sarveśvarī ('ruling over all') above.

Nine of these guardian spirits belong the nine individual chakras, and the last one (also known as Trikhaṇḍikā) belongs to the composite Śrī-chakra, pervading through all the parts.[12] The symbolism is also current that each of these guardian spirits rules over the six chakras in the body (*mulādhāra* at the base, *svādhisṭhāna, maṇipūra, anāhata, viśuddha* and *ājñā*), the *sahasrāna* (center of pure consciousness), the *laṁakāgra* (the centre of vision), and the bridge of the nose.

The three lines surrounding the square are taken to represent the feet, knees and thighs of Śrī-chakra personified as the deity. The divinity that presides over this enclosure (*chakreśvarī*) is Tripurā and the aids of the mother-goddess here are all manifest (*prakaṭa-yoginī*). The enclosure symbolises the first part of the emanation-chakra (*sṛshṭi-chakra*) denoting emanation-emanation (*sṛhti-sṛshti*).

2. *Second Enclosure,* called 'Fulfiller of all hopes' (*Sarvāśā-paripūraka*).

Its form is that of the lotus of sixteen petals (*shoḍaśa-patraka*), immediately within the three concentric circles (*tri-vṛtta*) and outside the lotus of eight petals. While delineating the petals, it is prescribed that there should be no space left between the petals. Such space is technically called 'keśara' (defined as 'dala-dvaya-madhyāvakāśa') which is said to spell harm.

The deity presiding over this enclosure is called Tripureśī, and her aids are unmanifest or hidden (*gupta-yoginī*). The powers that control this enclosure are sixteen in number, represented by the sixteen petals of the lotus from the East in counter-clockwise order : attractions pertaining to desire (*kāmākarshiṇī*), intellect (*buddhyā-*

karshiṇī), ego (*ahaṁkāra-karashiṇī*), sound (*śabdā-*) touch (*sparśā*), from (*rūpa-*) taste (*rasā*), smell (*gandhā*), thoughts (*chittā*), fortitude (*dhairyā*), recollections (*smṛtyā-*) verbal labels (*nāmā-*), sources of phenomena (*bājā-*) selfhood (*ātmā-*), immortality (*amṛtā*) and body (śarīrā-). They are indicated by the sixteen vowels, one inscribed on each petal, starting from East in a clockwise manner.

The corresponding center in the human body is *mūlādhāra-chakra,* the enclosure symbolize the second part of the emanation-chakra, denoting 'emanation-preservation' (*sṛshṭi-sthiti*).

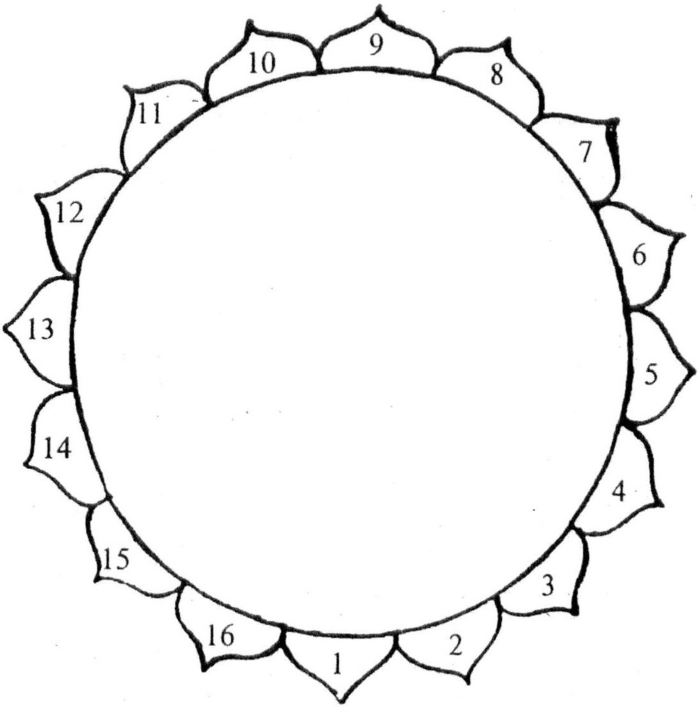

3. *Third Enclosure,* called 'Agitator of all' (*Sarva-saṅkshobhaṇa*)

Its form is that of a lotus having eight petals (*ashṭa-dala-padma*), immediately within the above enclosure and outside the main portion of the *yantra* (*viz.*, the complex figure formed by the inter-section of nine triangles).

The deity presiding over this enclosure is called Tripurasundarī, surrounded by her aids who are more hidden than the aids in the previous enclosure (*gupta-tara-yoginī*). The eight petals of the lotus represent eight forces which are psychophysical in nature (*anaṅga* meaning 'not entirely physical') : Anaṅga-kusumā (speech and expression, *vachana*) in the East, Anaṅga-mekhalā (apprehensions and

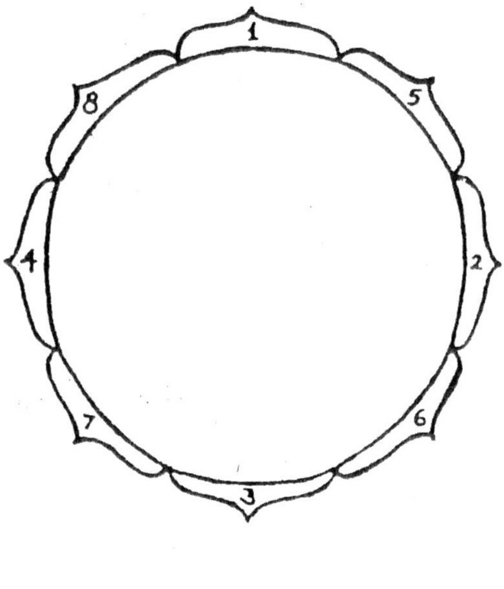
1
5
2
6
3
7
4
8

receptions, *ādāna*) in the South, Anaṅga-madanā (locomotions, *gamana*) in the West, Anaṅga-madanāturā (urges of the body and eliminations, *visarjana*), in the North, Anaṅga-rekhā (pleasureable feelings, *ānanda*) in South-East, Anaṅga-veginī (rejections and reactions, *hāna*) in South-West, Anaṅga-madanāṅkuśā (attention, *upādāna*) in North-West, and Anaṅga-mālinī (detachment and dispassion, *upekshā*) in North-East. They are indicated by the eight consonants beginning with 'ka'.

The corresponding center in the human body is the naval region (*nābhi*) or the loin (*kaṭi*).

The enclosure symbolized the third and final part of emanation-chakra, denoting 'emanation-absorption' (*sṛshṭi-saṁhāra*).

4. *Fourth Enclosure,* called 'Provider of all prosperity' (*sarvasaubhāgya-dāyaka*).

Its form is that of the fourteen-cornered figure (*chatur-daśāra*, or *bhuvana* standing for the fourteen realms, or Manu standing for the progenitors of the human race in fourteen segments of time), constituting the first enclosure in the main portion of Śrī-chakra (*viz.*, the complex figure formed by the intersection of nine triangles).

The deity presiding over this center is Tripura-vāsinī, surrounded by the aids 'conditioned by tradition' (*saṁpra-dāya-yoninī*).

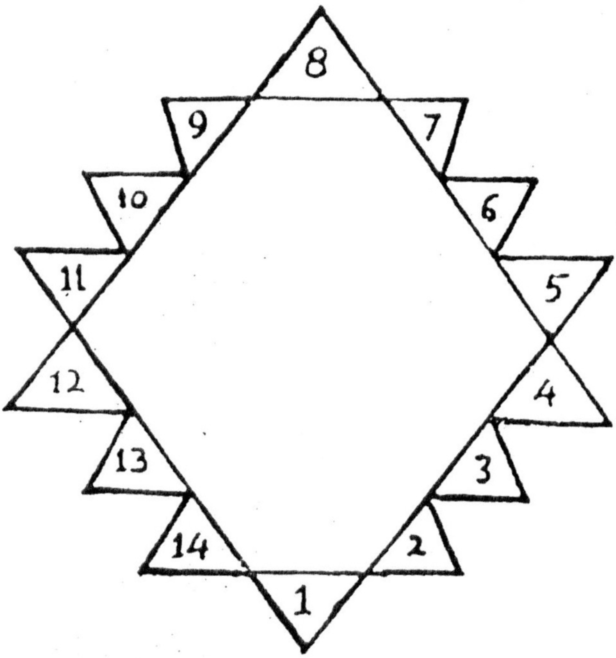

The fourteen corners (angles) of the enclosure represent fourteen of the vital channels (*nāḍī*) in the body. They are, from the East in anticlockwise order; Sarva-saṅkshobhiṇī ('agitator of all', *alaṁbushā-nāḍī*), Sarva-vidraviṇī ('chaser of all', *kuhū-*), Sarvākarshiṇī ('attractor of all', *viśvodarā*), Sarvāhlāda-kāriṇi ('delighter of all', *varaṇā-*) Sarva-saṁmohinī ('deluder of all', *hasti-jihvā-*), Sarva-stambhinī ('arrestor of all' *yaśo-valī-*), Sarva-jṛmbhiṇī ('releaser of all', *payasvinī-*), Sarvākarshiṇī ('attractor of all', alternately called Sarva-vaśaṁ-karī 'controller of all *gāndhāri-*), Sarva-rañjanī ('delighter of all', *pūshā-*), Sarvon-*mādinī* ('maddener of all', *śaṅkhinī-*) Sarvārtha-sādhanī ('accomplished of all objectives', *sarasvatī*), Sarva-sampatti-pūraṇī ('provider of all wealth', *iḍā-*) Sarva-mantra-mayī ('made up of all the *mantras*', *piṅgalā-*), and Sarva-dvandva-kshyaṁkarī ('destroyer of all duality', alternately called Sarva-dvandva-mayī, 'made up all phenomenal duality', *sushumnā-*). They are indicated by the first fourteen letters of the alphabet.

The corresponding center in the human body is the *anāhata-chakra* in the heart region.

The enclosure signifies the first part of the 'preservation'-chakra (*sthiti*), denoting 'preservation-emanation' (*sthiti-sṛshṭi*).

5. *Fifth Enclosure,* called 'Accomplisher of all objects' (*Sarvārthasādhaka*).

Its form is that of ten-cornered figure (*daśāra*), immediately surrounded by the above, it is specified as the 'outer ten-cornered figure' (*bahir-daśāra*), for it encloses another figure of the same nature.

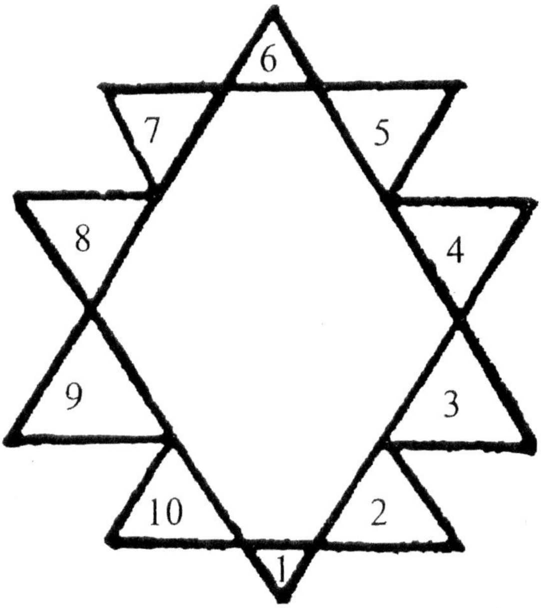

The deity presiding over this center is Tripurā-Śrī, surrounded by aids who are beyond the reach of sensory apprehension (*kulottīrṇa-yoginī*).

The ten corners of the figure house ten auspicious deities, from the East in anti-clockwise order; Sarva siddhi-pradā (ensuring all attainments), Sarva-sampat-pradā (bestowing all wealth), Sarva-priyaṁkarī (doing only the most desirable), Sarva-maṅgala-kāriṇī (bringing all the good things), Sarva-kāma-pradā (fulfilling all the desires), Sarva-duhkhavimochanī (removing all sufferings), Sarva-mṛtyu-praśamanī (counteracting all portents of death), Sarva-vighna-nivāriṇī (overcoming all obstacles), Sarvāṅga-sundarī (comely in all the limbs), and Sarva-saubhāgyadāyinī (gifting all prosperity). They are indicated by the five consonants beginning with 'ka' and the five consonants beginning with 'cha'. The number 'ten' also signifies the ten incarnations of Vishṇu, which secured the welfare of the worlds :

The corresponding center in the human bod is the *viśuddha-chakra* at the throat.

The enclosure signifies the second part of the 'preservation (*sthiti-*) chakra', denoting 'preservation-preservation' (*sthiti-sthiti*).

6. *Sixth Enclosure* called 'Protector of all' (*Sarva-rakshā-kara*).

Its form is that of a ten-cornered figure (*daśāra*) immediately inside the above, and therefore specified as 'inner' (*antar-daśāra*).

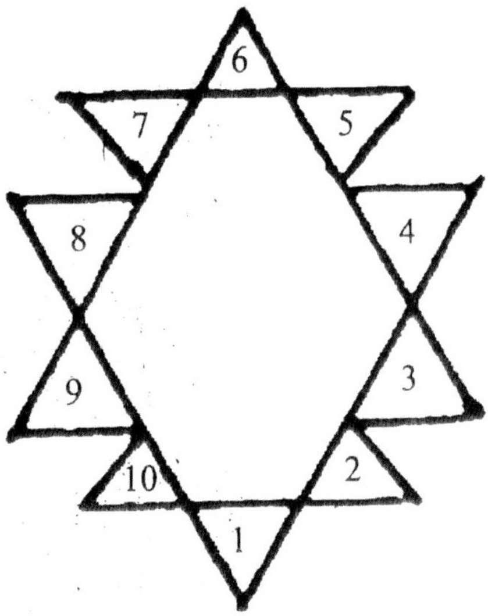

The deity presiding over this center is Tripura-mālinī, attended by aids who are 'embryonic' (*nigarbha-yoginī*).

The ten corners represent ten powers of the vital fire (*vahni-kalā*) : Sarvajñā ('knowing all', associated with *recha-ka,* elimination), Sarvaśakti-pradā ('bestowing all powers', *pāchaka,* digestion), *Sarvaiśvaryapradā* (bestowing all wealth', *śoshaṇa*, removing the defects of the stomachic fire), Sarva-jñāna-mayī ('full of all knowledge', *dāhaka,* burning), Sarva-vyādhi-vināśinī ('undoing all diseases', *plāvaka,* flooding with *rasa* to help the digestive function), Sarvādhāra-svarūpā ('supporting all things', *kshāraka,* bile-secreting), Sarva-pāpa-harā ('dispelling all misery', *ksho-bhaka,* churning food), Sarva-rakshā-svarūpiṇī ('protecting all beings', *jṛmbhaka,* yawning), and Sarvepsita-phala-pradā ('granting the fruits of all the one wants' *mohaka,* causing fainting). They are arranged in the corners from the East in an anticlockwise manner. They are represented by the five letters of the 'ta' group and give of the 'ta' group.

This figure is described as of the nature of fire (*agni*), and it symbolizes the third part of the 'preservation (*sthiti*) chakra, denoting 'preservation-absorption' (*sthiti-saṁhāra*).

The corresponding center in the human body is the maṇipūra-chakra, but it is said to be situated between the eye-brows.

7. *Seventh Enclosure,* called 'Remover of all diseases' (*Sarva-rogaharā*).

Its form is that of a eight-cornered figure (*ashṭa-koṇa*, also called *vasu-koṇa,* because the number of Vasus is eight). Its location is within the above enclosure and immediately outside the primary triangle.

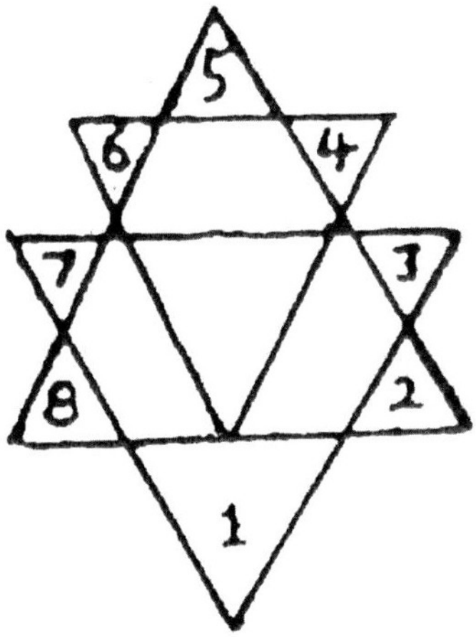

The deity presiding over this center is Tripura-siddhā, attended by aids who are described as 'secret' (*rahasya-yoninī*).

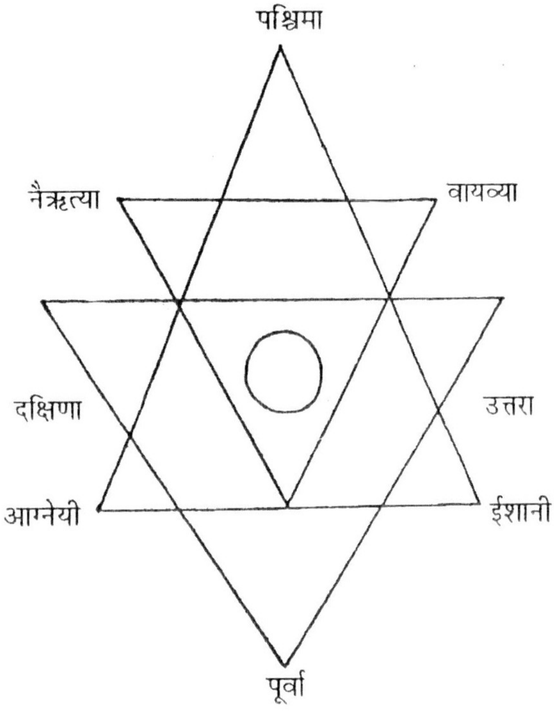

The eight corners represent the powers responsible for, or the expression of, the eight fundamental urges : Vaśinī ('subjugating', associated with *śīta,* cold), Kāmeśī (lording over desires', *ushṇa,* heat), Mohinī (causing confusing, or Mohinī, causing happiness, *sukha,* happiness), vimalā ('purifying', *duhkha,* pain), Aruṇa ('of the colour of ruddy dawn', *icchā,* desire), Jayinī (conquering', *sattva,* wisdom), *Sarveśī* ('lording over all' *rajas,* activity), and Kaulinī ('of the family' also called *Kula-sundari, tamas, inertia*), arranged in the eight-corners of the figure from the East in an anticlockwise manner. They are also described as 'deities of self-expression' (*vāg-devatās*) who are very close to the mother-goddess (Lalitā). The number eight symbolizes the eight forms that Śiva assumes (Rudra, Bhava, Śarva, Īśāna, Paśupati, Bhīma, Ugra, Mahādeva). They are represented

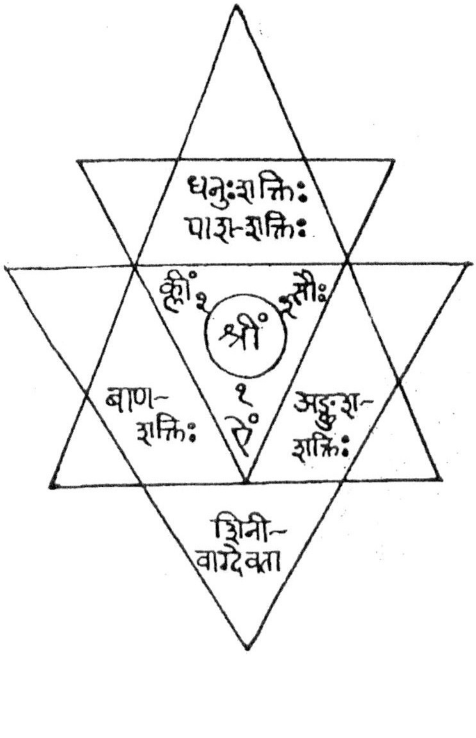

by the five letter of the 'pa' group and the letters 'śa', 'sa' and 'sa'.

The enclosure symbolizes the first part of the third chakra, 'absorption' *asaṁhāra-chakra,* denoting 'absorption-emanation' (*saṁhāra-sṛshṭi*). The corresponding area in the human body is said to be the forehead (*lalāṭa*), or alternately *svādhishṭhāna-chakra.*

Included in the same enclosure (in the space between this figure and the primary triangle) are four weapon-deities (*āyudha-devatā*) situated in the four directions guarding the primary triangle : Bāṇinī ('holding the arrow'), Chāpinī ('holding the bow') Pāśinī ('holding the noose') and Aṅkuśinī ('holding the goad').

8. *Eighth Enclosure,* called 'Bestower of all attainments' (*Sarvasiddhi-pradā*).

Its form is that of a triangle with the apex facing East (*viz.,* facing the devotee) or when drawn on paper, hanging downwards. This is the primary triangle, situated centrally and retaining an independence in structure. It is called Kāma-kalā, and is the immediate evolute of the central point (*bindu*).

The deity presiding over this enclosure is Tripurāmbā ('the mother of the triad') attended by aids who are 'exceeding secrets' (*ati-rahasyayoginī*).

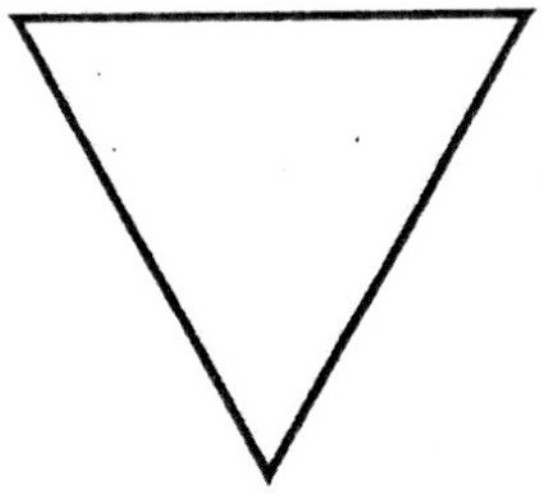

The three corners of the triangle represent three forms of the power of the mother-goddess: Kāmeśvarī (presiding over the Kāmarūpa-pīṭha; symbolizing Moon; representing Vāmā or the Vomiter of the expressive tendency, *viz.*, *Brahmā's* power of creation; and standing for the unmanifest aspect of Nature *viz.*, *avyakta-prakṛti*). In the eastern direction, Vajreśvarī (presiding over the Pūrṇāgiri-pīṭha; symbolizing Sun; representing Jyeshṭhā the first-born, *viz.*, Vishṇu's power by preservation; and standing for consciousness, *mahat*) to the right, and Bhaga-mālinī (presiding over the Jālandhara-pīṭha; symobolizing Fire; representing Raudrī or Rudra's power of dissolution; and standing for the ego, *ahaṁkāra*) to the left.

The three angles of the triangle also represent three forms of speech : paśyantī, madhyamā and vaikharī. The triangle is therefore called 'Speech-born' (*vāg-bhava*). The form of the triangle, representing the union of Śiva and Śakti, is suggested by the way in which the diphthong 'e' is written in Sanskrit. This vowel is formed by combining (*guṇa*) two vowel sounds 'a' (symbolizing Śiva) and 'i' (representing Śakti).[13] It is interesting to note that in the Guhyasamāja tradition of the Vajrayāṇa cult in Tibet also the letter 'e' symbolizes the 'triangle of Vidyā', comprehending the three-fold liberations: voidness, wishless and signless.

The triangle is also called 'wandering between horns' (*śṛṅgāṭa*), two horns seen in the two lines that meet at the eastern corner (facing the devotee) and the horizontal line touching these two lines on top suggestion movement between them.

The triangle is also called 'wandering between horns' (*śṛṅgāṭa*), two horns seen in the two lines that meet at the eastern corner (facing the devotee) and the horizontal line touching these two lines on top suggesting movement between them.

Regarded as the head (*mastaka*) of the mother-goddess, the figure is likened to *sahasrāra-chakra* in the human body. It is imagined that in the central space is situated the Uḍḍīyāna-pīṭha, the most important Tāntrika center. The mother-goddess, thus represented is 'three-fold in residence' (symbolizing the three Tāntrik centers Kāmarūpa, Pūrṇāgiri and Jālandhara, represented by three dots arranged to

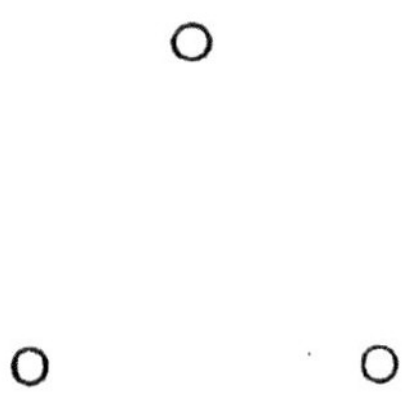

suggest a triangle), and in the empty space enclosed by the three in her unmanifest (hidden) abode (*Uḍḍīyā*). Kāmarūpa is the left-eye, Pūrṇāgiri the right-eye and Jālandhara the point between the eye-brows; the three units also symbolize the three fundamental tendencies of existence : desire (*icchā*), knowledge (*jñāna*) and activity (*kriyā*). Tripurā suggests not only the composite character but the unitary basis.

This center symbolizes the second part of the third chakra of absorption (*saṁhāra*), denoting 'absorption-preservation' (*saṁhāra-sthiti*).

The primary triangle, when taken to represent the iconic form of Lalitā (Rāja-rājeśvarī), the eight-cornered figure surrounding the triangle suggests the five basic elements of phenomenal existence (*tanmātra* : earth, water, fire, air and *ākāśa*), symbolized by the five arrows of flowers (*pañcha-bāṇa,* which is also the symbol of Kāma), passion (*rāga*) symbolized by the noose (*pāśa*), aversion (*dvesha*), symbolized by the goad (*aṅkuśa*), and mind (*manas*) symbolized by the sugarcane stalk (*ikshudaṇḍa*), all of which are held by the deity.

The primary triangle is white in colour, signifying pure *sattva.*

9. *Ninth Enclosure,* called 'Filled with all bliss' (*Sarvānanda-maya*).

Although called an 'enclosure', it is actually the point (*bindu*), which is central to the primary triangle (and to the whole pattern of Śrī-chakra). In fact, the primary triangle is merely the manifest form of the central point. The point is the actual *maṇḍala* or the abstract Uḍḍīyāna-pīṭha in which the mother-goddess resides (*bindu-maṇḍala-vāsinī, mahoḍyāṇapīṭhasthā*).

The deity that presides over the point-region (*baindavasthāna*) is Tripura-sundarī, Lalitā, Kāmakalā, Parā-bhaṭṭārīkā, Mahā-Kāmeśvarī or Śrī-vidyā. She is the empress of the entire kingdom of Śrī-chakra (Śrī-chakra-rāja-rājeśvarī). The aids that attend on her here are 'secret beyond all secrets' (*parāpara-rahasya yoginī*). This center is red colour, for it represents the deliberation of Śakti (*vimarśā*), spurt of activity (*rajo-guṇa*),[14] upon the foundational consciousness that the Śiva (*prakāśa*) (see section on the Tantra). The center thus is the 'field of deliberation,' which is the indissoluble union of the subjective and objective counterparts of experience, the 'I' and the 'This', *viz.*, Śiva and Śakti.[15]

In actuality, the central point is composed of three dots (or drops, *bindu-traya*), or three 'fires' : (*a*) Moon (*soma*), red in colour, representing the *iḍā* channel (or the left channel in the human constitution); (*b*) Sun (*sūrya*), white in colour, representing the *piṅgalā* (to the right vital channel; (*c*) and Fire (*vahni, agni*), of mixed colour and representing the central vital channel *sushumnā*.[16] The three dots are arranged in the form of a triangle.

The top dot symbolized the head of the deity as also the sign is Sanskrit for the unmodified nasal or *anuśvāra*, 'm', and the pair of dots at the bottom symbolized the breasts of the mother-goddess and also the sign for the unmodified sibilant or *visarga*, which also means 'creation', 'emanation', 'projection'. The two sounds are interesting, while producing the sound *m* (the unmodified or neutral nasal), we close the two lips together and the sound goes inward; while producing the other sound ('h', unmodified sibilant) we part the lips, and the sound goes out. The former illustrates the acts of 'gathering up' (*saṁhāra*) while the latter 'emanation' (*sṛsh-ṭi*).[17] The one central point becoming three is an act of 'swelling' (*ucchūna*). This is how the central point becomes the primary triangle in Śrī-chakra.

The center symbolizes the final part of the third chakra, of 'absorption' (*saṁhāra*) denoting 'absorption-absorption' (*saṁhāra-saṁhāra*). It is because of the complete absorption of the phenomenal projection into the very self of the mother-goddless and utter freedom from duality, the centre bears the name 'filled with all bliss.'[18] Bliss is defined as 'resting in oneself' (*svarūpa-pratishṭha*). In the human constitution, it corresponds to the central outlet within the *sahasrāra-chakra, viz., brahmarandhra.*

Complete absorption is another term for entirety (*sama-shtha, samasta*). That is why that mantra for the form of the divinity at this center is :

हूँ श्री समस्तां मूलविद्यां औड्डीयानपीठे
श्रीमहात्रिपुरसुन्दरी देवीश्रीपादुकां पूजयामि नमः।

REFERENCES

1. मिनोति क्षिपति उच्चत्वात् इति मेरुः।
2. cf. Buddha-guhya's gloss on *Durgati-pariśodhana-vṛti*. cf. also *Guhya-samāja-tantra*.
3. cf. *Ḍiṇḍima-bhāshya* on *Saundarya-laharī*, 24

cf. also, सृष्टिकर्त्री ब्रह्मरूपा गोप्त्री गोविन्दरूपिणी।
संहारिणी रुद्राख्या तिरोधानकरीश्वरी।
सदाशिवानुग्रहदा पञ्चकृत्यपरायणा।।
and सृष्टि स्थित्युपसंहारविधानानुग्रहात्मकः।
कृत्यं पञ्चविधं यस्य तन्नुमः शश्वतं शिवम्।।

(Śāmbhavī-dipikā)

4. श्रीवक्रं शिवयोवृपुः *(Lali ā-triśati)*

5. चतुर्भिः शिवचक्रैः शाक्तिचक्रै श्च पञ्चभिः।
नवचक्रैश्च संसिध्दं श्रीचक्रं शिवयोर्वपुः।।

(*Lalithā-triśatī*) also *Saundarya-laharī*. 11, and

पञ्चशक्तिचतुर्वह्निसंयोगाचक्रसम्भवः (*Sanketa-paddhati*)

6. त्रिधा चैव नवधा चैव चक्रसङ्केतकं पुनः। (*Yoginī-hṛdaya,* 1,73)

cf. also त्रिकोणं मण्डंल वरज्ञसर भूपुरं च त्रिरेखकं।
मन्त्रोऽपित्र्यक्षरः प्रोक्तः तथा रूपत्रयं पुनः।।
त्रिंविधाा कुण्डली शक्तिः त्रिदेवानां च सृष्टये।
सर्वं त्रयं त्रयं यस्मात् तस्मात् त्रिपुरा मता।। *(Kālikā-purāṇa)*

and नवायोनीवचक्राणि दधिरे नवैव योगा नव योगिनीश्च।
नवानां चक्रे अधिनाथस्योना नवमुद्रा नवभद्रा महीनाम्।।

(Tripuropanishat)

7. त्रिकोणमष्टकोणं च दशकोणद्वयं तथा।
चतुर्दशारं चैतानि शक्ति चक्राणि पञ्च च।।
बिन्द्वष्टदलं पद्मं पद्मं षोडशपत्रकं।
चतुरश्रं च चत्त्वारि शिवचक्राण्यनुक्रमात्।।

(*Lalitā-triśati, 'phala-stuti',* 12-14)

8. वामा ज्येष्ठा रौद्री चम्बिकयानुत्तराश भूताः स्युः।
इव्छाज्ञानक्रियाशान्ता श्चैतास्तथोत्तरावयवाः।। *(Kāmakalā-vilāsa, 23-24)*
बर्णिसेव आधारनवकस्थाः नवचक्रत्त्वेन परिणतिं याताः। *Ibid.* 47

9. त्रिकोणे बैन्दवं श्लिष्टं अष्टारेऽष्टदलाम्बुजं।
दशारयोः षोडशारं भुवनं भुवनात्त्मके।।

It is because of such union, which is six-fold, that the design itself is called 'yogini' (c.f. *Varivasyā-rahasya*, 2, 94).

शैवानामपि शाक्तानां चक्राणां च परस्परं।
अविनाभावसम्बन्धं यो जानाति स चक्रवित्।।

(*Bhairava-yāmala*, 'Chandra-jñāna-vidyā')

10. Śrī-vidyārnava-tantra.

11. एवमेतन्महाचक्रं महाश्रीत्रिपुरात्मकम्। (*Nityāpaṭala*)

12. सर्वस्य चक्रराजस्य व्यापिका परिकीतिता।

13. अकार: परमशिव:। तस्यस्त्रींसंयोग लक्षणे ङीप्। तयो: संयोगेन एकार निष्पत्ति:। (Bhāskara-rāya)

14. The three *guṇas* have their characteristic colours : *Sattva* or white, *rajas* red and *tamas* black.

15. वेदकवेधयो: अहंतेदंतयो: शाक्तीशक्त्यो: अभेदैवविमर्शाभूमिरेव बिन्दुचक्रमिति ज्ञेयम्।

16. cf. *Rudra-yāmala*, 6,49. See for furtehr details the section on the Tantra.

17. The idea of 'emission' in *visarga* is old as *Taittirīya-brāhmaṇa*, 3 (*Bhāvanopanishat*, 27)

18. सदानन्पूर्णा स्वत्मैव परा देवता। (*Bhavanopanishat*, 27).

Chapter 2

The Mantra of Śrī-Chakra

1. The Symbolism of Śrī-Chakra

One of the most interesting, if also intriguing, aspects of the Indian thought pertains to the philosophy of language. The raw materials of language are the sound-units that constitute the alphabet. The vowels from the short *a* to the unmodified nasal *ṁ*, fifteen in number, are regarded as the 'male' principle (Śiva), the foundational and contentless consciousness. From five of them *a* (अ), *i* (इ), *o* (ओ), *ṛ* (ऋ) and *lṛ* (ऌ), five groups of consonants (*viz.*, guttarals beginning with *ka* (क), palatals beginning with *cha* (च), cerebrals or unguals beginning with *ṭa* (ट), and dentals beginning with *ta* (त) and labials beginning with *pa* (प) evolve. The five consonants beginning with *ka* (क) represent the five primary forms of matter (the *mahābhūtas, viz.*, earth, water, fire, air and *ākāśa*); the five consonants of the *cha* (च) group represent the pure and bare condition of the same five forms (*tanmātras*); the five consonants of the *ṭa* (ट) group are symbolic of the five organs of action (*viz.*, speech, prehension, locomotion, excretion, and reproduction); the five consonants of the *ta* (त) group represent five sense-organs (visual, auditory, olfactory, gustatory and tactual); the five consonants of the *pa* (प) group stand for mind (*manas*), ego (*ahaṁkāra*), individualized consciousness (*buddhi*), the feminine principle of action, change and growth (*prakṛti*) and the masculine principle of undifferentiated but inspiring consciousness (*purusha*). Thus, these twenty-five consonants represent the twenty-five principles of existence (*tattvas*).

The other consonants are evolved from these five consonants : the liquid *ya* (य) and the sibilant *śa* (श) from *cha* (च); the liquid *la* (ल) and the sibilant *sa* (स) from *ta* (त); the liquid *va* (च) from *ta* (त) and *pa* (प) together; and the soft breathing *ha* (ह) from the unmodified sibilant at the end of vowel group (*visarga*). The four consonants *ya* (य) *ra* (र), *la* (ल) and *va* (व) represent the principles of attachment (*rāga*), wisdom (*vidyā*), *kalā* and *māgā;* and the four consonants *śa* (श), *sha* (ष), *sa* (स), *ha* (ह) represent the principles *mahāmāyā, śuddhavidyā, īśvara* and *sadāśiva.* Altogether, there are fifty letter (15 vowels and 35 consonants), and they exhaust the universe of existence and experience, of appearance and reality, of the empirical and the transcendental orders.

The universe bound by the dimension of its unmanifest origin (*Śiva*) on the one hand, and by the dimension of its manifest passing out and absorption (*Śakti*) on the other hand, are illustrated by the letters of the alphabet beginning with *a* (अ) and ending with *ha* (ह). The initial letter stands for the 'manifesting consciousness' (*prakāśa*) of Śiva and the final letter for the 'reviewing energy' (*vimarśā*) of Śakti.[1] The former is the 'origin' (*mūla*), while the latter is 'nature' (*prakṛti*). The universe, thus, is a play of the 'original nature (*mūla-prakṛti*), which is the mother-goddess (*mātā*). The letters of the alphabet, signifying the several forms of this 'original nature', are thus called 'mother-like' (*mātṛakās, 'mātā iva'*).

The Sanskrit word formed by the initial vowel '*a*' (अ) and the final consonant *ha* (ह) surmounted with the unmodified nasal (*ṁ*) means egoity ('I'), which pervades the entire world of experiencing and expressive living beings. It is important to note that the terminal consonant *ha* (ह) is associated with the last of the vowels, *ṁ*, thus suggesting the reassertion of *prakāśa* element. The symbolism of *aham* ('I') would therefore be Śiva-Śakti-Śiva. In fact, the entire group of fifteen vowels beginning with the soft '***a***' and ending with the unmodified nasal (*anusvāra, ṁ*) is counted as one principle, the first *tattva*.

In Śrī-vidyā ideology, there is no disparate existence of signifying sound (*vāchaka*) and the signified object (*vāchya*); and the expressing consciousness and the expressed energy are fundamentally one. The universe of experience, therefore, is nothing other than the expressive sounds that constitute the alphabet (*viśvaṁ vidyābhinnaṁ*). The thirty-six letters (the fifteen vowels taken as one, and the consonants 35) of the alphabet correspond to the thirty-six principles (*tattvas*) that underlie the constitution and function of the universe. The thirty-seventh principle (actually transcending the other principles, *tattvātīta*) is involved in an unmanifest manner for it is the necessary ground for the other principles which are manifest in the universe.[2]

The consonants by themselves are impossible to meaningful vocalize without the aid of vowels. The consonants as accommodated in the alphabet are, therefore, invariably associated with, in fact dependent upon, vowels (like *ka, la* etc.), as Śiva on Śakti. The vowels are said to provide power (*śakti*) to the consonants, which are in the nature of mere seeds (*bīja*).[3] To transform these ordinary letters into the 'mother-like' (*mātṛikā*) condition, the composite vowel power along with the thirty-seventh sound (corresponding to the unmanifest but present *tattvātīta*) is added. Technically, this additive detail is called 'the moon and the point' (*chandra-bindu*), the moon signifying the collective power of fifteen vowels tending towards the final unmodified nasal, and the point (dot) suggesting the twenty-seventh principle. Moon's parallelism with the fifteen vowels taken collectively is derived from the fact that moon has fifteen phases (*tithi*) during each fortnight, the sixteenth phase being transcendental and unchanging.[4]

The letters of the alphabet are also identified with various aspects of the divnity. The vowels constitute the head, *a* and *ā* the back of the head and face, *i* and *ī* the two eyes; *u* and *ū* the ears; the *ṛ* and *ṛṛ* nostrils, *lṛ* and *lṛṛ* the two cheeks; *e* and *ai* the two sets of teeth, upper and lower; *a* and *au* the two lips; the unmodified nasal (*ṁ*) the tongue, and the unmodified sibilant *ah* (*visarga*), the neck. The consonants constitute the rest of the body; the *ṭa*-group and the *ta*-group feet; the *pa* and *pha* the two arm-pits; *ba, bha* and *ma* tactile sensations, navel and heart. The other consonants are vital currents inside the body.

The articulated awareness in the form of sounds meant to obtain, crystallize and communicate knowledge concerning the most fundamental principles governing the universe, is in the Tantrik lore designated *Vidyā,* It consists essentially of individual letters of the alphabet, and specific sounds when articulated. *Vidyā* thus means not only verbal knowledge but the underlying conceptual reality. The term *vidyā* is generally employed to mean an aspect of the mother-goddess. The tantras speak of ten such mother-goddesses (*daśa-Vidyās*) who are identified with different sound-patterns and their symbolisms : Kālī, Tārā, Shoḍaśī,

Bhuvaneśvarī, Bhairavī, Chinna-mastā, Dhūmavatī, Mātaṅgī, Kamalā and Bagalāmukhī. Of these ten, the first two are described as *mahā vidyās*, the next five as *vidyās*, and the last three as *siddha-vidyās*. The first group of *vidyās* is meant for few and advanced devotees, the second for most of the devotees, and the third for devotees intent on magical skill and violent results.

The third of these *Vidyās* is known as *Śrī-vidyā,* also known as *Shoḍaśī,* because the *mantra* of this mother-goddess consists of sixteen letters with the addition of the sacred seed-syllable 'Śrī.' A variant of this *mantra,* however, comprises only of fifteen letters (with the omission of the terminal Śrī), known as *pañchadaśī*. This *vidyā* is a peculiar arrangement of letters (vowels and consonants) in three units, which signify the thirty-six (in *pañchadaśī* or thirty-seven in *shoḍaśī*) principles that we mentioned already. That it is the verbal formulation of the visual Śrī-chakra will be discussed later.

2. Pañchadaśī and Shoḍaśī

The universe of fifty letters (*mātṛakā-chakra*) is accommodated in the rays of light (*kalā*) which sustain the universe : the vowels are the 16 aspects of the Moon (15 for the days of the fortnight, and the transcendental aspect which is beyond change), the consonants from *ka* are the 24 aspects of the Sun; and the consonants from *ma* are ten aspects of Fire.[5] Thus the *mātrkā-chakra* comprises three fields (*tri-purā*), three types (*tri-vidhā*), or three parts (*tri-khaṇḍā*). Hence the mother goddess who symbolizes this triad is Tripurā. She also signifies the three powers that confirm her presence; power of cognition, the power of action, and the power of intention.[6] In her aspect as the power of cognition, she is designated as Vāgiśvarī (the field being called *Vāgbhavachakra*); in her aspect as the power of action, she is Kāmeśvarī (the field being called *Kāmarāja-chakra*); and in her aspect as the power of intentions she is Parā-śakti (the field being called *Śakti-chakra*).[7]

In the iconic representation of the mother-goddess, the first field (Moon) is regarded as her head, the second (Sun) as her torso, and fields are fifteen 'mother-like' letters, which collectively are called Pañchadaśī (or Shoḍaśī, with the addition of another seed-letter *Śrī*) is not merely the *mantra* of the mother-goddess; it is itself the mother-goddess, even as the ninefold *yantra* is itself the body of the mother-goddess. The origin of the mantra is traced back to the *Śāṅkhāyana-Śruti*.

The tradition that advocates the use of this *mantra* mentions twelve pioneers : Manu, Chandra, Kubera, Lopāmudrā, Manmatha (Kāma), Agastya, Nandi, Sūrya, Vishṇu, Skanda, Śiva and Durvāsa (Krodhabhaṭṭāraka). Many of these names do not suggest historical persons, except Lopāmudrā, Agastya and Durvāsa. Different versions of the same *mantra* are said to have been taught by others like Dharma-rāja, Agni, Nāga-rāja, Budha, Brahmā, Īśāna, Rati (wife of Kāma), Jīva, and Varuṇa.[8] These versions are extant, but they are not in vogue. The only versions that popularly prevail are those associated with Agastya ('Kādi' version) and his wife Lopāmudrā ('Hādi' version). All version alike take the human in Sāṅkhāyana-śruti as their common authority.

The hymn[9] cited produces this mantra of fifteen letters in three groups, known as *kūṭas* (peaks) or *khaṇḍas* (sections).

1. क उ ई ल। ह्री[9]।

2. ह स क ह ल। ह्री[9]।

3. स क ल। ह्रीं।

This version, which begins the *mantra* with the letter *ka* is known as 'kādi-vidyā' ('the formula commencing with *ka*). There is another version, which omits some letters and gives letters in a slightly different order :

1. ह स क ल। ह्रीं।

2. ह स क ह ल। ह्रीं।।

3. स क ल। ह्रीं।।

This alternate version commences the *mantra* with the letter *ha* and is therefore known as 'hādi-vidyā' ('the formula commencing with *ha*). The former tradition, said to have been promulgated by Kāma (Eros), is ascribed to a line of teachers: Parama-śiva, Durvāsa, Hayagrīva and Agastya; and it is more popular all over the country than the other one. *Tantra-rāja-tantra* and *Vāmakeśvara-tantra* are its chief authorities. The latter tradition goes back to Lopāmudrā, wife of the sage Agastya, and was prevalent in Kerala. The main text on which this tradition relies is *Tripuropanishat.* There is a belief that the 'Kādi' tradition is not only earlier but more important.[10]

There are several other versions of the *mantra,* depending upon the main import that is sought to be projected. That a group of five versions, known as *pañcha-sundarī,* was prevalent at one time has been mentioned in some medieval texts :

1. Verbal communication (*bhāshā*) :
   ह क ल स। ह्रीं। क ह ल स। ह्रीं। क ल स ह। ह्रीं।।
2. Emanation (*sṛshṭi*) :
   ह स क ल। ह्रीं। ह ल क ह स। ह्रीं। स क ल। ह्रीं।।
3. Preservation (*sthiti*) :
   ह ल क स। ह्रीं। क स ह ल। ह्रीं क ह स ल। ह्रीं।।
4. Absorption (*samhṛti*) :
   ह ल क स। ह्रीं। क स ह ल । ह्रीं। ह ह क ल। ह्रीं।।
5. indeterminate state (*nirākhyā)* :
   ल क स। ह्रीं। स ह क ल। ह्रीं। ह स स ह क। ह्रीं।।

Another version, designed to gather up thoughts and make the mind inoperative in the normal framework but active in the spiritual practice (unmanī) has been mentioned:

क ए ई ल । ह्रीं । ह क ह ल । ह्रीं ।
ह स क ल । ह्रीं

Only two among the versions, however, have been in vogue among the general run of practitioners : 'kādi' and 'hādi.' The difference between the two versions is mainly in the number of effective letters used. When the repetitions of the letters are not counted, the 'kādi' version has seven letters (क ए ई ल ह्रीं ह स), while 'hādi' has only five (ह स क ल ह्रीं). The latter omits two letters *e* and *ī*, both of which are held as very important in the 'kādi' tradition. That is why the 'kādi' tradition, adopted by one of the most important among the texts of Śrī-vidyā, *viz.*, *Lalitātriśatī-stotra*, is held in high esteem.[11]

There is another view which emphasizes the primacy of one or the other of the three units in the fifteen-lettered mantra. The view known as Kālī-krama (also *Kuṇḍalī-krama*) begins the *mantṛa* with the unit क ए ई ल। ह्रीं। (and hence designated *kādi-vidyā*); it underlines the *sattva* (benevolent, knowledge-oriented) aspect of the mother-goddess. In terms of the *pañcha-sandhyā* ritual, the mantra is worshipped as Kāmakalā-kālī at dawn, as Bhuvaneśvarī at noon, as Chāmuṇḍā at dust, as Samaya-kubjikā at night and as Kādi-pañchadaśī at midnight. This is prescribed as most suitable for householders. The view known as *Tāra-krama* (also called *samavarodhinī-karma*) begins the mantra with the unit स क ल । ह्रीं, (and hence *sādi-vidyā*), emphasizing the *rajas* (dynamic, action-oriented) aspect of the mother-goddess. In the *pañchasandhyā* ritual, she is worshipped as Dakshiṇā-kālī (or Aniruddhāsarasvatī) at dawn, as Tārā at noon, as Bāla at dusk, as Jñāna-sarasvatī at night, and as Sādi-pañchadaśī at midnight. The third view known as *Sundarī-krama* (also called *Haṁsa-krama*) begins the mantra with the unit ह स क ह ल । ह्रीं। (and hence *hādi-vidyā*), and emphasizes the *tamas* (malevolent, ignorance-oriented) aspect of the mother-goddess, who is worshipped as Ādyā-kālī at dawn, Tārā at noon, Chinna-mastā at dust, Bagalā-mukhī at night, and Hādi-pañchadaśī at midnight. The last one is said to be suitable only for those engaged in black magic, sorcery and such other evil mechanizations. Householders are forbidden to adopt either the Tārā or the sundarī-krama.

What has been said till now refers to the fifteen-lettered *mantra* of Śrī-vidyā as *pañcha-daśi*. But an older tradition speaks of 'Shoḍaśī' (the *mantra* with sixteen letters, figuratively described as 'the girl of sixteen') as the real Śrī-vidyā.[12] It is not only praised as the best of *vidyās*, but great secrecy is attached to it : "Do not impart to the undeserving this sixteen-lettered lore, even if you are threatened with death. This lore must be guarded as a great secret like one's private part. When the devotee's mind becomes absorbed in the feet of the *guru,* like salt in water, it is only then that the great *vidyā* is to be communicated to him, out of compassion."[13] This is said to be the hidden import of all the Vedas, *śāstras, purāṇas* and the *yāmalas.*[14]

But the *shoḍaśī* is substantially the same as *pañcha-daśī*, using the same letters in the same order, but adding the seed-syllable of prosperity 'Śrīṁ' at the end.[15] The form it would take would be :

ओँ । क ए ई ल। ह्रीं । ह स क ह ल । ह्रीं ।
स क ल । ह्रीं । श्रीं॥

But then, the nature of the *mantra* would significantly alter. Instead of the three units (*khaṇḍas*) of the *pañchadaśī*, we have here four units, 'Śrīṁ' itself constituting the fourth unit, called 'transcendental unit' (*turīya-khaṇḍa*). In the *pañchadaśī* the transcendental form is said to be subtle or unmanifest, whereas in the *shoḍaśī it becomes explicit.*[16] Thus, instead of the thirty-six *tattvas* expressed in the *pañchadaśī*, the *shoḍaśī*, speaks of the thirty-seventh *tattva* beyond *tattvas* also.[17] The expression 'Śrī-vidyā' refers to the importance of this ultimate but pervasive principle represented by the syllable 'Śrī'.

The mother-goddess has only fifteen aspects, corres-ponding to the fifteen phases of the moon in the fortnight; but the sixteenth aspect that the *shoḍaśī* includes is pervasive in all the phases and is verily the entirety of the mother-goddess, in her natural aspect as pure existence, conscious-ness, and bliss.[18] *Pañchadaśī* also enumerates this as the transcendental aspect (*turīya-kūṭa*), but more by implication than by explicit statement. The explanations of the *mantra* of fifteen letters always reckon four units, the fourth, however, not including any letters of the *mantra*.

· There are also extensions of *pañchadaśī* like the ones into the seventeen-lettered *mantra* (*saptadaśa-vidyā*), with at the end, *humsa* in *Rudrayāmala,* into the eighteen-lettered *Kāmarāja-ashṭadaśa-vidyā* with the initial addition of *aim* in the first unit, *hrīṁ* in the second, and *śrīṁ* in the third (ऐं क ए ल ह । ह्रीं । ह्रीं ह स क ह ल । ह्रीं । श्रीं स क ल । ह्रीं ॥), into the twenty-one-lettered *mantra* in *Siddha-yāmala* (क र ई ल । ह्रीं। ह स क ह ल । ह्रीं। स क ल । ह्रीं । स्त्रीं ऐ क्रो क्रील्कां । हू ॥) and into the thirty-seven-lettered *para-vidyā* :

ओं । ऐं क्लीं सौः। क ए ल ह ह्रीं । सौः क्लीं ऐं ।

ओं । ऐं क्लीं सौः । क स क ह ल ह्रीं । सौः क्लीं ऐं ।

ओं । ऐं कलीं सौः । स क ल । ह्रीं । सौः कलीं ऐं। ओं॥

There is also a *mahā-shoḍaśī* with 28 letters : eight seed-syllables, *pañchadaśī* (15 letters) and the first five seed-syllables in the reverse (*viloma*) order.

In all these instances, the basic structure is that of *pañchadaśī,* and care is always taken to group the letters and other seed-syllables into three explicit units, with the fourth unit either spelt out or implied. Even when absent or undefined, the fourth unit it is that endows unitary significance on the *mantra.* The three explicit units are like unto the body of the mother-goddess ("*mūla-kūṭa-traya-kalevarā*", *Lalitā-sahasranāma*), while the implicit fourth is her very self. Seed-syllables like *aim, klīṁ* and *śrīṁ* emphasize this fourth unit, which is regarded as 'secret' (*rahasya*).

Bhāskara-rāya, the most revered authority on the Śrī-vidyā, roundly tells us that "those who merely know how to articulate the *mantra* without understanding the meaning thereof are like donkeys carrying loads of sandal-wood; utterance of words without a knowledge of their import will not tend to any accomplishment, even as ghee poured on the ashes will not help light a fire."[19] And he suggests that meanings are manifold : general sense, tradition I import, secret teaching, practical import, etymological meaning, explanations based on word-power, total meaning etc. "In short, there are as many meanings as there are letters in the *pañchadaśī*"[20]

Broadly, however, meanings are two-fold : (1) explanations of the essential symbolism and verbal imagery involved; and (2) communications of practical significance, meant to guide the devotee. The latter are of course, beyond the scope of this (or any other) book. The former two are both elaborate and diffuse; and much of the imagery has now become obsolete. Works of comparatively recent origin which seek to offer symbolic explanations for the *mantra* can be forbiddingly complex, abounding in flights of imagination (like *tri-kāṇḍa-sārārtha-bodhinī, Śrī-vidyā-saṇketa-bhāshya* and *Pañchadaśī-rahasya-vivaraṇa*). But works of celebrated writers like Gauḍapāda, Lolla-Lakshmīdhara, Bhāskara-rāya and Gīrvāṇendra-sarasvatī attempt to perfect the traditional view-point that it is the primal symbolism (*ādi-vidyā*) which provided the inspiration for the Vedas and the rest of religious and philosophical lore in the country ('sarva-veda-śāstrāṇām api kāraṇa-bhūtā'). There may be some truth in the argument that this symbolism goes back to hoary antiquity.

Pañchadaśī has, as has often been mentioned earlier, fifteen letters arranged in three units (*khaṇḍas* or *kūṭas*).

The first unit is called *Vāgbhava-kūṭa* and contains five letters. The first letter, guttaral *ka,* stands for Kāmeśvara, the higher principle that governs our intentions and desires; it stands for the field of waking life, where the sense-organs and mind are transacting with the phenomenal world outside (*jāgradabhimānī-viśvah*). The letter is explained as derived from the root which means 'to illumine' (*kan dīptau*); and in this sense, it is the principle of consciousness (*buddhi*). It is also the vital principle in the human constitution, and it is the symbol of Self.[21] Finally, *ka* is said to represent 'kāma', the cosmic urge to find expression and satisfaction, or Brahmā the creator. The consonant *ka* is actually a union of the sound *k* with the vowel *a* (Śiva-Śakti).

This is an important letter, as it occurs thrice in the *mantra*. It is said that it suggests three kinds of devotees (*upasakas*), sakala (impure, inferior, believing only in actions), 'pralayakalā' (mixed, midling, believing in actions as well as knowledge), and 'vijñāna-kevala' (pure, superior, believing in knowledge only).[22]

The second letter is *e,* which, stands for the feminine counterpart of the above, Kāmeśvarī or Lakshmī. The symbol *e,* which resembles a triangle when written in Sanskrit, typically stands for the mother-goddess as the source of all things.[23] It is derived from the root which means 'to remember' (*īk smaraṇe*), and represents the dream state, where the mind is dynamic (*svapnābhimānī taijasah*). If *ka* is Brahmā *e* is the power of Brahmā to manifest, express and denote (Bhāratī).

The central point (*bindu*) enclosed in a triangle (*trikoṇa*), which signifies the consonant *ka* followed by the vowel *e,* symbolizes the union of Śiva and Śakti which is responsible for the emanation, preservation and dissolution of the phenomenal world, as suggested in the opening verse of *Saundarya-laharī*. The former (Śiva) is represented by one half of the *yantra* (composed of four triangles), while the latter (Śakti) is represented by the other half (composed of five triangles). Together they bring about all the nine enclosures that go to constitute the whole *yantra*.[21] There is also an explanation that Śiva represents the Vedāntic Absolute (*avikṛta-chaitanya, brahman*) and Śakti the power of *māyā*, the union of the two being responsible for the world.[25] In the Sāmkhyan framework, the union of Purusha and Prakṛti is the corresponding ideology.[26] The central point (*bindu*) is in poetic imagery styled as the 'ocean of ambrosia' (*sudhā sindhu*), within the 'abode of the wish-fulfilling crystal (*chintāmaṇi-gṛha*) *viz.*, the triangle, surrounded by the *nīpa*-trees (*viz.*, the lines of the *yantra*).

The third letter *ī* stands for Vishṇu for the etymological significance of the roots of the two are the same (*īyate vyāpnoti*). Pervasion of consciousness throughout experience is indicated by the involvement of the state of deep sleep with this symbol (*sushuptyabhimānī prājñah*). It is also referred to as Māyā, the power of cosmic projection and concurrent ignorance of the reality. The letter *ī* is said to resemble a dark cave, which covers, encloses and hides.[27]

The fourth letter *la* stands for earth (*kshiti*), the principle that remains isolate from the sensory activity in waking, from mental processes in dream, and suggests insensibility to perception (*paroksha*), beyond the phenomena, and uninvolved.[23] The letter *la* is actually a symbol of the essential condition of phenomenal existence. That is why it occurs thrice in the *mantra*, suggesting its hidden relevance for the three worlds.

The seed syllable *hrīṁ* which comes at the end of this group of four letters is not a part of the first unit, but a 'crowning of peak'. *Hrīṁ* is an especially sacred syllable representing the mother-goddess herself. It is a composite sound, consisting of the seed-letter *ha* (meaning 'sky' or 'void') the sound *r* (*repha* signifying 'fore'), and the terminal letter *ī* (Manmatha), closing with the unmodified nasal *ṁ* (*anusvāra* suggesting dissolution). The first constituent *ha* is said to be white in colour, the second constituent *ra* red in colour, and the third constituent *i* blue in colour. The three constituents thus represent the three *guṇas* (*sattva*, *rajas*, and *tamas*), which are indistinguishably dissolved in the mother goddess as *mūla-prakṛti*. A second explanation is also given : *ha* stands for Śiva, *ra* for Śakti, and *i* for their union resulting in utter tranquility.

The same seed syllable (*hrīṁ*) is repeated at the end of the second and the third units. Technically *hrīṁ* is called the 'streak from the heart' (*hṛllekhā*), *viz.*, ardent aspiration of the devotee. This is also considered as the one-lettered *mantra* of Māyā or Bhuvaneśvarī (who not only governs the three worlds but withdraws them into herself). The etymological significance of *hrīṁ* is 'bashful' : the phenomenal world as yet withdrawn (*saṅkocha*) is in a state of hiding in her, but it has all the potentialities of unfolding and manifesting. The seed-syllable, which is extensively employed in Tāntrik rituals is described as the tāntrik equivalent of the Vedic *Om* (*tāntrika-praṇava*). It gives the sense of completion : the letters in each unit of the *mantra* are separate by themselves (*vyashṭi*), but the employment of *hrīṁ* at the joints (*kūṭa*) transforms them into a unity (*samashṭi*). That is why the position of *hrīṁ* is figuratively described as 'knot' (*granthi*), the first being *brahma-granthi*, the second *Vishṇu-granthi* and the third *Rudra-granthi*.

The terminal sound *ṁ* (*bindu, anusvāra*) has along with it the crescent moon (*ardhachandra*) and the invisible powers (*rodhini, nāda, nādānta, śakti*), which are present only when the seed-syllable is articulated, and not when written. This complex seed-syllable is identified with the supreme mother-goddess (*para-devatā*), whose presence and power are sought to be packed into the *mantra*. The import of each preceding letter is imagined as flowing into the succeeding one, and the imports of the entire series to coalesce in the terminal *hrīṁ*.

The first unit, called *Vāgbhava-kūṭa* is so called because the unit is presided over by the creator both of the material world and of the linguistic forms, Brahmā. And its importance is derived from the fact that it includes the three most important seed-syllables : *ka* from which everything arises and which confers on the devotee the highest benefit of liberation; *la* which brings to the devotee unfailing prosperi- ty; and *ī* which secures all happiness. Thus, this unit is the very substance of the entire Śrī-vidyā, which in its turn is the epitome of all religious lore.[29]

The first *kūṭa*, according to the 'hādi' tradition, is obtained by replacing the first three letters (*ka, e, ī*) by the sixth (*ha*), the seventh (*sa*) and the first (*ka*) of *Kādi-pañchadaśī*.

Bhāskara-rāya tries to draw out the significance of the famous *gāyatrī* hymn from this unit of *pañchadaśī* : *ka* standing for "tat", *e* for "savitur vareṇyam", *ī* for "bhargo devasya dhī", and *la* for "mahi." The third quarter of the hymn, being meant by the peak symbol *hrīṁ*, which also includes the inarticulated fourth quarter.[30]

The second unit, called *Kāmarāja-kūṭa*, contains six letters (*ha, sa, ka, ha, la, hrīṁ*), three of which (*ka, la, hrīṁ*) are repetitions from the first; and one letter (*ha*) is repeated twice in this unit. The two new letters are *ha* and *sa*. The letter *ha*, when it occurs as the initial letter of this unit, means 'to strike', 'to destroy' (*hanyate*, destruction of the five kinds of bondage and evil); it represents Sun in this context. When the same letter occurs again, it means 'to obtain', 'to reach' (*hīyate, prāpyate*) all that one desires, it stands here for the divine Swan (*haṁsa*) (from the root *ohāṅg*, 'to go'.)

The other new letter *sa* is taken to signify helping to enjoy pleasures, mundane and spiritual (*sīyante*, from *so, 'to enjoy'* or *sū* 'to procreate'); it represents the cool rays of the Moon. The letter *la* (which is also found in the first unit) means here 'plenty' (*ādhikya*), when taken along with the final peak-syllable *hrīṁ* (*viz., lahrīṁ, laharīṁ*). The syllable *hrīṁ* in the second unit, however, has the same significance as in the first.

The third unit, called *Śakti-kūṭa,* has four letters (*sa, ka, la, hrīṁ*) all of which are repetitions from the first or second units. The three letters (*sa, ka, la*) taken together, however, mean 'entirety' (*sakala*), *viz.*, all the *tattvas* from the transcendental Śiva to the phenomenal earth (*sa* is symbol for Śakti, and *la* for the earth).

Of the letters that go to form this *mantra, ka* occurs twice and *ha* occurs twice; they signify the Male ingredients (Śiva). The other single letters all belong to the Female (Śakti). The composite seed-syllable *hrīṁ*, which occurs thrice, is both Male and Female.[31]

The three units are representatives respectively of the three cosmic powers; Fire, Sun and Moon;[32] the three gods, Brahmā the creator, Vishṇu the preserver, and Rudra the destroyer; three supreme values of human life, *dharma* (life in accordance with divine law), *artha-kāma* (walth and pleasures), and *moksha* (the final freedom from phenomenal involvement); the three aspects of the Vedic lore, *Rgveda,*

Yajurveda and *Sāma-veda;* the three linguistic arrangements (*cchand.ı*), *gāyatrī*, *trishṭup* and *jagatī.*

Each of the units has its own characteristic and collective seed-syllable : *aiṁ* for the first, *klīṁ* for the second and *sauh* for the third. The three together constitute the sound-body of the mother-goddess. Hence the *gāyatrī* for Tripurā takes the following form :

ऐं त्रिपुरादेव्वै विद्महे। क्लीं कामेश्वयैं च धीमहि।
सौः तन्नः क्लिन्ना प्रचोदयात्॥

The first unit (represented by *aiṁ*) is the head of the mother-goddess Tripurā; the second unit (*klīṁ*) constitutes her body from the neck below till the waist; and the third unit (*sauh*) is the portion of her body below the waist. In

the human body, the unit (*aiṁ*) is the Fire that starts from the basal plexus (*mūlādhāra*) and rises till the *anāhata* in the heart-region; the second unit is the Sun that rises from the *anāhata* and touches the *ājñā* centre between the eye-brows; and the third unit is the Moon that emerges from the *ājñā* centre and touches the top of the forehead (*lalāṭa*).

The *pañchadaśī* with the above three *kūṭas* are to be regarded as the stream of sound that rises from the basal *mūlādhāra* centre and goes right up to the thousand petalled lotus on the crown of the devotee's head. This sound passes through the three 'peaks' (*kūṭas*) symbolized by the sound *hrīṁ*, as a thread through three beads of a rosary.[33]

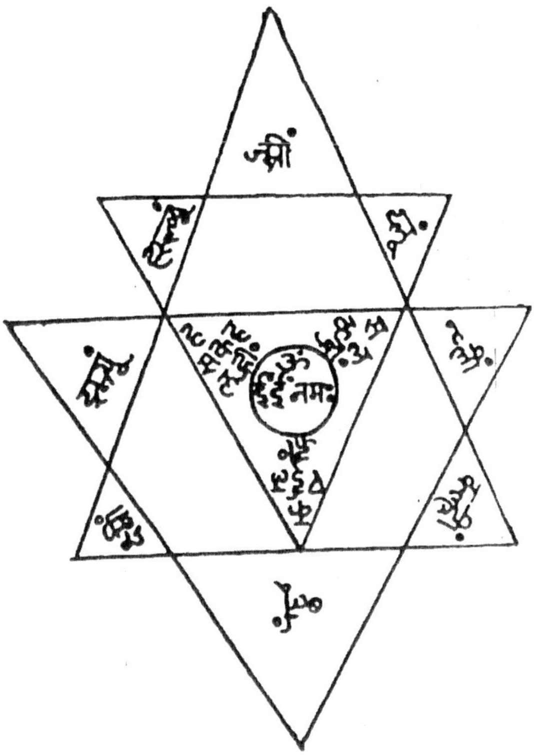

3. Identity of Yantra and Mantra

Works on Śrī-vidyā insist on the conceptual identity of the visual representation in the form of Śrī-chakra with the verbal imagery that is known as *Śrī-vidyā-mantra* (fifteen-lettered *pañchadaśī* or sixteen-lettered *shoḍaśī*). The two are used conjointly in worship rituals, and each has its own thematic specificity and procedure of employment. But the prevailing idea in the entire worship is that the two are basically of one nature, one form and one import.

The expression 'Meru' (Sumeru) applies equally to Śrī-chakra and to the *Śrī-mantra.*[34] The expression is derived from the ancient mythical lore, common to many Asian countries, that in the centre of the universe is the most resplendent mountain, made of solid gold and studded with jewels on the slopes, soaring unimaginably high, and that it has three peaks, on the middle of which the heavens are located; the three peaks are said to be the residence of three gods : of Brahmā on the Western peak, of Vishṇu on the eastern peak, of Śiva on the central peak; the base of the mountain is square in shape, each side being differently coloured; and the fourteen worlds are arranged around the base.[35] It is the king of mountains, and the beings that dwell on it are free from sorrow, old age, disease and death. In the Tibetan lore Meru is the mountain located in the middle of the milky ocean, rising high on a base of four sides, having fights of steps on each side made of gold, silver sapphire and amber; alround the base are grown the wish-granting trees (*kalpa-vṛksha*) decorated with a thousand victory banners fluttering in the breeze. The mountain faces east; and the four continents surround the base. The three peaks of the mountain represent the three diamonds (*vajra*) : body, speech and thoughts.[36]

Śrī-chakra is a representation of the Meru mountain, the King of mountains (*chakra-rāja*), and the idea of three peaks (*tri-kūṭa*) dominates over this conception. Each peak formed like a triangle has three sides; and on each side is a *chakra*. Thus there are altogether nine *chakras, yonis* or enclosures entering into the structure of *Śrī-chakra*. The *mantra* appropriate to Śrī-chakra also has three parts (*tri-khaṇḍa*), corresponding to the three peaks of the *yantra*. There are again, nine letters (*navārṇa*) in the *mantra* corresponding to the nine enclosures (*navāvaraṇa*) of the *yantra;* and they exhaust the entire universe. Thus the *mantra* also is a *meru.*[37]

The mantra of *Śrī-chakra* is significantly called *mātṛkā-chakra,* the pattern of seed-letters, arranged, as already explained, in three units representing Moon (Soma), Sun (Surya) and Fire (Agni).[38] The supreme deity that presides over the mantras as well as the yantra is Tripurā, the goddess of three fields. The triad is the dominant motif : the three individual units and the union of the three as the fourth (*turīya*). The three comprehend all the details of the world and spiritual practice, and the fourth (implicit in each of the three) is the highest objective of spiritual endeavour.

The primary triangle (*koṇa-traya*) in the *yantra* along with the central point (*bindu*), as the fourth detail, is regarded as the initial seed-letter *aim* (*e,* representing the triangle as explained the previous section, along with the *bindu*), from which the entire *mantra* evolves. The letter *e* itself is the symbol of union of Śiva (*a*) and Śakti (*ī*). The form of the diphthong *e* in Sanskrit is enough to establish the identity of the *yantra* and *mantra,* which are imagined to represent Śiva and Śakti respectively. The central point (*bindu*) like the unmodified nasal *ṁ*, is beyond concrete representation or explicit vocalization. It is regarded as the 'fourth' (*turīya*), implicit in the three concrete units of the triangle. The three units in both the *yantra* and the *mantra* are called *chakras* (or *kūṭas,* or *khaṇḍas*).

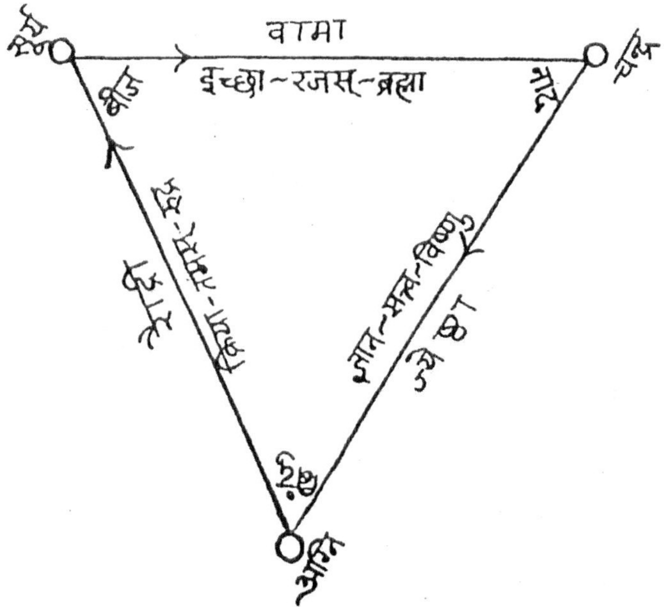

The three *chakras* are : Fire, Sun and Moon, with Brahmā (formless) as the fourth. The three corresponding institutional directions (*amnaya* or *samayas*) are East, South and West, with North as the fourth; the spiritual centres (*pīṭhas*) in them are respectively Kāmarūpa, Pūrṇāgiri and Jālandhara, as Uḍḍīyāna as the fourth; and the three presiding deities Kāmeśvarī, and Bhagamālinī respectively with Mahā-tripurasundarī as the fourth. The three powers (Śakti) are : Vāmā (with her consort Brahmā), Jyesṭhā (with her consort Vishṇu) and Raudrī (with her consort Rudra), with Śāntā ('tranquil') as the fourth; corresponding, to these are desire (*icchā*, associated with Bharatī, spouse of Brahmā), knowledge (*jñāna* associated with *kshiti,* spouse of Vishṇu) and action (*kriyā,* associated with Aparṇā, spouse of Rudra). The three principles (*tattva*) are : Self (*ātmā*), liberating wisdom (*vidyā*), and the ultimate good (*śiva*), with entirety (*sarva*) as the fourth. The three selves are : individual self (*ātmā*), the inner self (*antarātmā*) and the highest self (*paramātmā*), with the enlightened self (*jñānātmā*) as the fourth. The conditions of the individual self are three : wakefulness, dream and deep sleep, with *turīya* as the fourth. The cognitive process (*puṭa*) also involves three units : the knower (*jñātr*), the knowledge (*jñāna*) and the known (*jñeya*), with their perfect union (*sāmarasya*) as the fourth. The verbal expression (*śabda*) is three-fold : cognizable although indistinguishable (*paśyantī*), distinguishable but inarticulate (*madhyamā*), articulate, expressive and suggestive (*vaikharī*), with 'transcendental' (*parā*) as the fourth.

It may be recalled that the different parts of the Śrī-chakra are inscribed with different groups of letters of the Sanskrit alphabet, each letter symbolizing an aspect of the power of the mother-goddess. In the tradition of *kailāsa-prastāra* layout, Śrī-chakra symbolizes the identification of 50 letters (*mātṛka*) with the mother-goddess. The two decorative parts, *viz.*, the surrounding square (*bhūpura*) and the peripheral triple girdle (*tri-vṛtta*), are left out in such inscription. In each of the petals of the sixteen-petalled lotus (*shoḍaśa-patraka*), one of the sixteen vowels is inscribed, *a* at the eastern entrance, and moving in sequence in the anti-clockwise manner. On the petals of the eight-petalled lotus (*ashṭadala-padma*), groups of consonant letters are inscribed from *ka* to *ksha*. The vowels are forms of Śakti, and consonants of Śiva : thus these two lotuses by themselves signify the conjunction of Śiva and Śakti.

The enumeration of the letters of the alphabet is continued, one letter in each corner, in the fourteen-cornered figure (*chaturdaśāra*) inwards till the eight-cornered figure (*ashṭa-koṇa*). The eight-cornered figure is inscribed with composite seed-syllables; and the primary triangle (*mūlatri-koṇa* or *Vāgbhava*) has in each of its corners a unit (*khaṇḍa*) of the *pañchadaśī-mantra,* the first unit in the eastern corner, facing us when kept horizontally (or at the apex below when held vertically) the second and third units in the two corners on the right and to the left of the apex. The central point is usually left uninscribed, because it is beyond both visual representation and verbal expression. When, however, the point is made to swell into a circle (*ucchūna* condition), the foundational male seed-syllable '*Om*' and the seed-syllable specific to the mother-goddess *īṁ* are inscribed.

There is an account of how each of the nine *chakras* in the *yantra* is evolved from the letters included in the fifteen-lettered *mantra, pañchadaśī.*

From the latter *ka* occurring thrice in the *pañchadaśī* and signifying the powers of desire, knowledge and action, and from the letter *ī* which together represent the union of *kāma* and *kalā*, the central point (*bindu*) evolves; this is the first *chakra*. Two subsequent *chakras* (primary triangle and the eight-cornered figure) arise from the complex seed-syllable *hrīṁ*. The next three *chakras* (comprising the 'preservation aspect' (*sthiti*) evolve from the letter *ha* occurring twice and from the letter *e* respectively., The two peripheral *chakras* (the two lotuses) are derived from the letter *sa* occurring twice. The final *chakra*, (*viz*., the surrounding square) evolves from the letter *la*, occurring thrice in the *mantra*.[39]

Each of the chakras has also a specific ***mantra*** :

1. *bhūpura* : अं आः सौः।
2. *shoḍaśa-patraka* : ऐं क्लीं सौः।
3. *ashṭa-dala-padma* : ह्रीं क्लीं सौः।
4. *chaturdaśāra* : हैं हस्कीं हसौः।
5. *bahirdaśāra* : हसौ ह्सौं हस्क्लीं क्स्सौः।
6. *antardaśāra* : ह्रीं क्लीं ब्लें।
7. *ashṭa-koṇa* : ह्रीं श्रीं सौः।
8. *tri-koṇa* : ह्स्त्रौं क्स्कल्रीं ह्स्स्त्रौः।
9. *bindu* : *pañchadaśī* or *shodaśī*

REFERENCES

1. अकारः सर्ववर्णाग्र्यः प्रकाशः परमः शिवः।
हकारोऽन्त्यः कलारूपो विमर्शाख्यः प्रकीर्तितः।।
अतोऽकार-हकाराभ्यां अहमित्यपृथक्तया।
प्रपञ्चं शिवशक्तिभ्यां क्रोडीकृत्य प्रकाशते।।
2. Cf. *Varivasyā-rahasya. 2.*
3. Cf. ककार दि क्षकारान्ता वर्णास्ते शिवरूपिणः।
अकारादि विसर्गान्ता स्वराः षोडश शक्तयः।।
शिवशक्तिमया वर्णाः शब्दार्थप्रतिपादकाः।
शिवः स्वरपराधीनो न स्वतन्त्रः कदाप्यसौ।। (*Māṭṛkā-maṇḍala*)
also देवता मातृका देवी बीजं व्यञ्जनसञ्चयं।
शक्तयस्तु स्वरा देवि षडङ्गन्यासमाचरेत्।। *Kñānārṇava*
also समस्त मातृकायास्तु हला बीजानि शक्तयः।
स्वराः स्युः परमेशानि जात्या व्यक्ति तु कीलकः।।

अनिर्वाच्यानां हलां स्वरसंयोगेन सुवाच्यता etc. (*Uttara-tantra*)

4. *Kāma-kalā-vilāsa*, 17

नित्यास्तिथ्याकारास्तिथयश्च
शिशक्तिसमरसाकाराः॥

cf. also दर्शाद्याः पौर्णिमान्तश्च कलाः पञ्चदशैव तु।
षोडशो तु कला ज्ञेया सच्चिदानन्दरूपिणी॥

Śiva is likened to the moon's digit that is visible (*darśākhyā chāndrī kalā*) and Śakti to the digits that make the moon visible (*drishṭākhyā kāla*) cf. comm. on *Saundarya-Lahari*, 1

(*Aruṇāmodinī*)

5. षोडशेन्दोः कला मानोद्विर्द्वादश दशानले।
सा पञ्चशत्कला ज्ञेया मातृकाचक्ररूपिणी।

6. त्रिपुरा त्रिविधा देवी ब्रह्मविष्ण्वीशरूपिणी।
ज्ञानशक्तिः क्रियाशकिरिच्छाशक्त्यात्मिका प्रिये॥

(*Vamakeśvara-tantra*)

7. धागीश्वरी ज्ञानशक्तिर्वाग्मवे मोक्षरूतिणी।
कामराजे क्रियाशक्तिः कामेश्वरी कामरूपिणी॥

शक्तिबीजे परशक्तिः कामेश्वरी कामरूपिणी।
एवं देवी त्र्यक्षरी तु महात्रिपुरसुन्दरी॥

8. cf. *Śrī-vidyārṇava-tantra*, 7, section on 'Śrī-vidyāyāh bhedānā-muddhārah', pp. 114-115.

9. cf. 'Prakāśa' on *Varivasyā-rahasya*. The following hymn is cited as the mnemonic description of the *mantra*:

The expantions of the words used :

कामों योनिः कमला वज्रपाणिर्गुहा हसा मातरि श्वाभ्रमिन्द्रः।
पुनर्गुहा सकला माया च पुरूच्येषा विश्वमाताऽऽदिविद्या॥

कामः (Eros) = क; योनिः (Source) = ए; कमला (goddess) = ई; वज्रपाणिः (Indra) = ल; गुहा (Skanda) = ह्रीं; हसा = हस; मातरिश्व (air) = क; अभ्रं (Sky) = ह; इन्द्रः = ल; again गुहा = ह्रीं; सकला = स क ल; माया = ह्रीं

10. कादेः प श्चादेव हादेरुद्धारः।

11. तत्र कादिर्यथा परा।

12. *e.g. Jñanārṇava,* 24, 28

षोडशार्णा परा विद्या श्रीविद्यत्यमिधीयते।

cf. also *Siddha-yāmala*

कामो माया रामा बाला त्रिकूटा च भगाङ्कुशो।
काली कामकला कूर्चः सर्वादौ प्रणवः प्रिये।
श्रीमहाषोडशीयं च या ख्याता भुवनत्रये।
ज्ञानेन मृत्युहा सर्वाग्नायैर्नमस्कृता।।

13. *Ibid.* 68-69.

न देया षोडशार्णा हि प्राणैः कण्ठगतैरपि।
गोपितव्या महाविद्या स्वयोनिरिव पार्वति।।

उदके लवणं लीनं यथा भवति शैलजे।
मनों भवति विलीनं मादयोः श्रीगुरोः प्रिये।
तदा देया महाविद्या कृपया षोडशाक्षरी।।
राज्यं देयं शिरों देयं न देया षोडशाक्षरी।।

14. *Ibid.*, 64.

वेदशास्त्रपुराणेषु य मलेवंपि गुता षोडशर्णा etc.

15. षोडशाचरी तु श्रीबोजावसाविनी पञ्चदश्यैव।

16. पञ्चदश्यां तुरीयस्वरूपा पञ्चदशो सूक्ष्मरूपेण विराजते।

17. Cf. *Kāma-kalā-vilāsa,* 18

षद्त्रिंशतत्त्वात्म तत्त्वातीता च केवला विद्या।

18. cf. *Subhagodaya.*

दर्शाद्याः पूर्णिमान्ता पञ्चदशैव तु।
षोडशो तु कला ज्ञेया सच्चिदानदरूपिणी।।

19. *Varivasyā-rahasya,* 2, 54, 55

20. *Ibid.,* 59

21. ककारस्य आत्मवाचित्वात्।
22. cf. *Svacchanda-saṅgraha* :

    अशुद्ध शुद्धमिश्राणां प्रमातृणां परं वपुः।
    क्रोधोश त्रितये न स्य विद्यास्थेन प्रकश्यते।।
23. यदेकादशमेकार बीजं कोणत्रयात्मकम्। *(Chatuh-śatī)*
    also उद्धोलः कामरूपश्च एकारश्च त्रिकोणकः। (*Cātṛkā-kośa*)
24. त्रिकाणरूपी शक्तिर्बिन्दुरूपः शिवः स्वयंः।
    अविनाभा सम्बन्धस्तस्म द्बिन्दुत्रिकोणयोः।।
    उभयस्यास्य देवस्य विग्रहे यन्त्रकल्पना।
    विना यन्त्रेण चेत्पूज देवता न प्रसीदति।।
25. cf. *Padārtha-chandrikā* on *saundarya-laharī*, 1.
26. cf. *Ḍīṇḍima-vyākhyā* on *Saundarya-laharī,* 1.
27. ईकारस्य गुहावचित्वादविद्यारूपतया तदवच्छिडन्नत्वात्।
28. अविद्यातस्कार्यसम्बन्धविच्छेदनादसङ्गस्तुरीयः।
29. *Śrī-krama*, 3, 4.

    ककारे सर्वमुत्पन्नं कामकैवल्यदायक।
    लकारे सकलैश्वर्य ईकारे सर्वसौख्यदं।।
    एवं बीजत्रयं देवि विद्यानां सारसङ्गहं।
    वाग्भवं कामराजं च शक्तिं तेन नियोजयेत्।।
30. *Varivasyā-rahasya.* 1, 43
31. कद्वयं हद्वयं चैव शैवो भागः प्रकीर्तितः।
    शत्त्कत्यक्षराणि शेषाणि ह्रींकार उभयात्मकः।।
32. त्रिखण्डं मातृकाचक्रं सोमसूर्यानलात्मकम्। (*Rudra-yāmala*)

    Sometimes the three units are called Soma-khaṇḍa, Sūrya-khaṇḍa and Agni-khaṇḍa.
33. *Varivasyý-rahasya,* 1, 21.
34. त्रीचक्रमपि देवेशि मेरुरूपं न संशयः।
35. cf. *Bhāgavata,* 5, 16, *Matsya-purāṇa,* 95, 7 and *Narasiṁha-*, 30, 14, 46.

36. cf. Ratnākara-śānti's *Meru-maṇḍala,* in Tibetan, *Mandal-gyi-choga.*

37. नवाक्षरो मेरुरयं ब्रह्माण्डगोलकः।

38. त्रिखण्डं मातृकाचक्रं सोमसूर्यानलात्मकम्।
महालक्ष्म्याः पुरं चक्रं तत्रैवास्ते सदाशिवः।। (*Rudra-yāmala*)

39. *Varivasyā-rahasya,* 2, 99, 100
कत्रितयादीकाराद्बिन्दुर्जातः तदग्रिमे चक्रे।
हल्लेखाभिस्तत्परचक्रत्रितयं हकाराभ्यां।।
एकारेण च तत्परचक्रे जाते सकाराभ्यां।
चतुरस्राणि लकारैः एवं विद्याक्षरेण चक्रजनिः।।

Chapter 3

The Tantra of Śrī-Chakra

श्रीचक्रं श्रुतिमूलकोश इति संसारचक्रात्मकं।
विख्यातं तदधिष्ठिताक्षरशिवज्योतिर्मयं सर्वतः।
एतन्मन्त्रमयात्मिक भिररुणां श्रीसुन्दरीभिर्वृतं।
मध्ये बैन्दवसिहंपीठललिते त्वं ब्रह्मविद्या शिवे॥

(Durvāsa)

1. Śrī-Vidyā

Śrī-vidyā is a cult of considerable antiquity, comprehending a *yantra* (*viz.*, *Śrī-chakra*), a *mantra* (*viz.*, *Pañchadaśī* or *Shoḍaśī*), and a *tantra* (*viz.*, *Śrī-Vidyā*). It is prevalent all over the country, although there are regional variations in the tradition. The *mantra* and the *tantra* thereof are not quite as popular as the *Śrī-chakra*, which is familiar not only to devotees but also to the art enthusiasts. While the actual worshippers of *Śrī-chakra* are few in number, those who reverence it and keep copies of the sacred diagram either in print or in metal in their homes or places of work are in large numbers. The mere presence of *Śrī-chakra* (even without a ritualistic worship to it) is believed to confer on the faithful material and spiritual benefits.

There are several temples, especially in South India, where the worship of *Śrī-chakra* assumes an important detail.

Among them are the temples at Kāñchīpuram *(Kāmakoṭi)*, Chidambaram (*Sammelana-chakra*), Jaṁbukeśvaram (*Lalitā*), Kūrtālam, Avaḍaiyyār-koyil, all in Tamiḷnāḍu, Śṛṅgeri (*Śāradā*) and Kollūr (*Mūkāṁbikā*) in Karṇāṭaka. There is a legend, without however any foundation, that the great Śaṁkara installed a *Śrī-chakram* in the famous temple at Tirumala-Tirupati, and that the unparalleled prosperity of the temple is to be ascribed to this reason. Inspired by this legend, several temples have begun to utilize the Śrī-chakras. There is a temple in Karṇāṭaka (Chandalā-Parameśvarī shrine in Sannati in Gulbarga district) which has the *vimāna* on the sanctum shaped like a huge *Śrī-chakra*.

There can be little doubt that the cult of *Śrī-chakra* has a tāntrik background, although efforts are made to relate it to the Vedic tradition. That there were two traditions in the country since very ancient times, *viz.*, Tāntrik and Vedic, has been recognized even by the staunch votary of Vedic orthodoxy, Kullūka-bhaṭṭa (who lived between 1150 and 1300 A.D.).[1] The two naturally involved themselves in rivalry and conflict, but they compromised and interacted equally naturally. The present-day religious ideas and practices in India represent amalgums and fusions of the two traditions in various proportions and degrees. The cults relating to the mother-goddess and female tutellary deities belong to the Tāntrik tradition; the rituals involved in them clearly reveal this background, although symbolisms and interpretations have been in many cases borrowed from the Vedic thought-structure.

Śrī-chakra is essentially worship of the mother-goddess called Lalitā, Tripurā-Sundarī, Shoḍaśī, Rāja-rājeśvarī or merely Devī. Her consorts (*devatās*) and aids (*yoginī*) are also female, and they too receive worship as 'retinue-divinities' (*parivāra-devatās*). The ritualistic details are also characteristically femine in emphasis. The diagrammatic representation involves the basic form of triangle, the typical symbol of feminity (*yoni*). A degenerate cultic variation recommends the worship of the actual generative organ of the chosen female (*pratyaksha-yoni*) as the living *Śrī-chakra!*

The mother-goddess cult in India has crystallized the concept of 'energy-centres' (*śakti-pīṭhas*) associated with places. The mother-goddess who dominates the Śrī-chakra cult is associated with as many as fifty centres in her various forms and aspects, spread all over the country. Twelve of them have been popular : Kāñchīpuram (Kāmākshī), Nepāl (Kumāri), Gurjara (Aṁbā), Mālavā (Kālikā), Prayāga (Lalitā), Vārāṇasī (Viśālākshī), Vindhyāchala (Vindhya-vāsinī), Gayā (Maṅgalā-Chaṇḍī), Baṅga or Calcutta (Sundarī), Karavīra or Kolhapur (Mahā-Lakshmī), Assām (Guhyeśvari), and Malaya mountains (Bhrāmarī). However, it is in the Kāñchīpuram shrine that the Śrī-chakra cult was active and persistent. It was from here that the cult spread all over the southern part of the country.

Despite the fact that great secrecy was attached to the worship of the mother-goddess in the Śrī-chakra form, a fairly rich literature has grown up on the subject. But this literature does not go back beyond the sixth century, although some of the works (like *Bhāvanopanishat* and *Aruṇopanishat*) are couched in archaic style. Much of the literary source material is to be found included in Tāntrik texts dealing with all aspects of the cults (principally *Vāmakeś-vara-tantra, Yoginī-hṛdaya-tantra, Śakti-saṅgama-tantra* and *Svacchanda-tantra*), as well as in the manuals based on them but dealing with specific issues (like *Rudra-yāmala, Tripurārahasya, Kāmakalā, Setubandha, Nityā-shoḍaśikā-kalpa, Paraśurāma-kalpa* and *Varivasyā-rahasya*). While most of the Tāntrik texts are products of the ninth and tenth centuries, the manuals were much later productions, some of them as recent as the eighteenth century.

The tendency noticeable in many of these manuals is to reconcile the cultic ideas derived from the Tantra with the Vedic tradition. Lolla-Lakshmīdhara, for instance, claims that Śrī-vidyā is actually derived from *Taittirīya-āraṇyaka* (1, 11, 54; 1, 12, 32; 1, 23, 1; 1, 32, 127), and tries to draw parallels between the Vedic *yajña* and the rituals of *Śrī-vidyā*. *Bhāskara-rāya*, to cite another instance, derives *Śrī-vidyā* from a hymn in *Ṛgveda*[2] and *Śrī-chakra* from another.[3] It is also claimed that *Śrī-vidyā* is an evolved form of the celebrated Vedic hymnal deity Gāyatrī (cf. *Śrī-vidyā-mantra-bhāshya, 'Trikāṇḍa-sārātha-bodhinī,* Veerarāghava-śāstrī).

Śaṁkara, the reputed advocate of Vedic authority, is claimed in legendary accounts to have been initiated in the tāntric cult of *Śrī-Vidyā* at Banaras. The principal poetic work in this cult, *Saundarya-laharī*,[4] is ascribed (wrongly, however) to his authorship; a part of this work is said to have been recovered by him from Kailāsa. He is also said to have composed a general work on tāntrik worship, *Prapañcha-sāra*, a cultic text on Tārā-worship (*Tārā-prābhratikā*) and a hymn to a tāntrik deity (*Chintāmaṇi-stava*, according to Bhāskara-rāya). His teacher, Gauḍapāda, is also claimed to have written two manuals on Śrī-vidyā (*Śrī-vidyā-ratna-sūtra* or *Śakti-sūtra* according to Bhāskara-rāya) and *Subhagodaya-stuti* on which there is a commentary by Lolla-Lakshmīdhara). And his teacher, Govinda is said to have been the author of a general tāntrik work, *Jayadratha-yāmala*, which was discovered in Nepāl. The Śrī-Vidyārṇava accounts of the lineage of Śrī-vidyā teachers includes all the important names of the Vedic tradition : Kapila, Atri, Vaśishṭha, Sanaka, Sanandana, Bhṛgu, Sanatsujāta, Vāmadeva, Nārada, Gautama, Śaunaka, Śakti, Mārkaṇḍeya,...Parāśara, Śuka,...Vyāsa,... Gauḍapāda,... Pārāśarya, Satyanidhi, Rāmachandra, Govinda, and Śaṁkara. From Śaṁkara onwards the lineage continues through Padmapāda (who wrote *Sambhandha-dīvikā*, a gloss on *Prapañcha-sāra* ascribed to Śaṁkara), Bodha, Gīrvāṇa, Ānanda, Vishṇu-śarmā, Pragalbha and Vidyāraṇya.[5]

The association of Śaṁkara (author of the *Bhāshyas* on *Brahmasūtra, Bhagavad-gītā* and the *Upanishad*) with tāntrik cults is very uncertain, and the above account of his tāntrik lineage can scarcely be trusted. His acquaintance with *Śrī-vidyā*, if indeed there was any, is not even faintly suggested in his Vedāntic writings. He appears to have been entirely ignorant of *Śrī-chakra*, if we rely on his well-known works. Yet it is remarkable that the pontificates that claim to have been founded by him make him a devotee of Śrī-chakra. However, these pontificates have encouraged the cult of Śrī-chakra, and have contributed considerably to the spread of the cult.

It is probable that Vidyāraṇya (who is regarded as a teacher in Śaṁkara's line) was proficient in the Śrī-chakra cult. A treatise on this cult, *Śrī-Vidyārṇava-tantra* is ascribed to his authorship. Associated with the founding of the Vijayanagar empire (around 1336 A.D.) and with two pontificated Kāñchīpuram and Śṛngeri (both owing allegiance to Śaṁkara), he was a great spiritual, social and political force in South India. It may be due to his influence that the *Śrī-vidyā* cult spread in this part of the country. His disciple, Lakshmaṇa-deśika, who performed a *devīyāga* in the capital of the Vijayanagar empire, must have striven hard to reconcile the *devī*-ideology of the tāntrik tradition and the *yāga*-prescriptions of the Vedic tradition. He is the author of a general tāntrik work of considerable celebrity, *Śāradā-tilaka,* along with its supplement *Tāra-pradīpa*. His disciples are supposed to have popularised the Śrīvidyā cult in different parts of the country : Mallikārjuna in the Vindhyā region, Trivikrama in Orissa ('Jagannāth') Śrīdhara in Bengal (Gauḍa Mihila and Vaṅga) and Kapardi in Banaras and Ayodhyā.[6] It was he who provided the literary framework for Śrī-vidyā in the four works : *Tantra-rāja-tantra, Mātṛkār-ṇava, Tripurārṇava* and *Yoginī-hṛdaya.*[7] It may safely be assumed that the present ideological and ritualistic strictures of the cult were crystallized by him.

The glory of the Vijayanagar empire reached its peak during the reign of Kṛshṇa-deva-rāya (1509-1529 A.D.). Along with the political fortune of the Hindus, the revival and spread of the traditional values of the Hindu culture also took place. It was in this context that the cult of Śrī-vidyā gathered momentum. Lolla-Lakshmīdhara, who was one of the leading scholars in the court of Kṛshṇa-deva-rāya, was the son of Viśvanātha-bhaṭṭāraka (who bore the title 'Modern Vyāsa', *nūtanavyāsa*) in the court of Vīrarudra, the Gajapati ruler of Orissa. Lakshmīdhara was also in the Orissa court (or Pratāpa-rudra) before Kṛshṇadeva-rāya ascended the throne of Vijayanagar. He wrote a lucid and authoritative commentary on *Saundarya-laharī* (ascribed to the great Śaṁkara), and a brief gloss on *Subhagodaya-stuti* (ascribed to Śaṁkara's teacher, Gauḍapāda). The former work became the chief source-material for the later writers of Śrī-vidyā. It has remained to this day an indispensable guide for the students of this cult.

Another name associated with the Vijayanagar court as well as the spread of *Śrī-vidyā* cult is that of Gambhīra-rāya-dīkshita, who however retired in his later years to Vārāṇasī. His son, Bhāskara-rāya (initiatory name Bhāsurānanda-nātha) was a polymath and he undertook to revive the tāntrik aspects of *Atharva-veda,* which had been lost in oblivion at that time. He was a *Śrī-vidyā* enthusiast and wrote extensively (in Sanskrit). The most significant among his works are *Setu-bandha* (a commentary on *Vāmakeśvara-tantra,* written in 1733 A.D.), *saubhāgya-bhāskara* (a commentary on *Lalitā-sahasra-nāma,* included in *Brahmāṇḍa-purāṇa*) (1778), *Varivasyā-rahasya* (with his own gloss entitled *Prakāśa*), *Ratnāloka* (a commentary on *Paraśurāma-kalpa-sūtra*) *Guptavatī* (a commentary on *Durgā-sapta-śatī,* included in *Mārkaṇḍeya-purāṇa*) and *Bhāshya* on the *Bhāvanopanishat.* He also wrote works on Vedic literature, grammer, prosody, Nyāya, Smṛtī, Vedānta and Mīmāṁsā; he was also a poet.

A South Indian settled in Vārānasī, a brilliant scholar in the Vedic and Tāntrik lores and an indefatigable advocate of *Śrī-vidyā,* he had ample opportunities to examine the cultic presuppositions and practices current in different parts of the country, to reconcile them, and to revitalize the essential aspects of the cult. It was he who crystallized the tāntrik point of view of *Śrī-vidyā*. He recognized the need on the part of some of the devotees to resort to the cruder forms of external worship,[8] and the need, on the part of the more advanced devotees, to dispense with the physical and external approach altogether and to worship *Śrī-chakra* as manifested in the human constitution itself.[9] During his day, Tantra had become disreputable by degenerate cultic practices, especially of the 'left-handed sect'. Bhāskara-rāya attempted to clarify the real Tāntrik outlook, and clear numerous misgivings.[10]

Both Lolla-Lakshmīdhara and Bhāskara-rāya sought to reorient the cult not only to accommodate the Vedic ideas but to eschew the degenerate practices that had become almost natural and necessary part of the cult. They minimized the value of external rites and practices and emphasized the merit of 'inner worship' (*antar-yāga*), once a fair degree of understanding has arisen. They underlined the prescription given by the *Vāmakeśvara-tantra* (51) :

अन्तर्यागात्मिका पूजा सर्वपूजोत्तमा प्रिये।
बहिः पूजा विधातव्या यावज्ज्ञानं न जायते॥

"Best of all forms of worship is inner worship. External worship (*viz.*, ritualistic) is to be resorted to until the dawn of enlightenment."

2. The Primal Model

Both the *yantra* and the *mantra* of Śrī-vidyā emphasize that the universe is an integrated structure, and that the integrity of the structure derives from the functional unity, or the unity of direction which in turn is due to the presence and power of the mother-goddess. The *yantra* is a concrete model of this integrated pattern, organization of parts in a whole, total unity that is not disturbed by the presence of manifold shapes or multitudinous projections. The same principle is held applicable to the individual constitution (*piṇḍāṇḍa*) also.

Tantra being a practical discipline, its concern is more with the individual than with the universe. It holds that the individual contains within himself all the essential dimensions of the universe; and that the entire universe unfolds itself in the development of the individual. If the universe represents diffusion and separation (*vyashṭi*), the individual represents focussing and compactness (*samashṭi*). The presence and the power of the mother-goddess could, therefore, be discerned more markedly in the individual.

The Tantra ideology, as is well-known, works with the human model of *chakra*-organization. The human constitution, in its essential and abstract structure, consists of six centers of organization : *mūlādhāra* at the base of the spinal column (*meru-daṇḍa*), *svādhisṭhāna* just below the navel region, *maṇipūra* around the navel region, *anāhata* at the heart, *viśuddha* at the throat, *ājñā* between the eye-brows. These are taken to correspond with the six directional deities (*āmnāya-nāyikās*). In group of two, they represent the three aspects the mother-goddess, whose presence it is that renders all these *chakras* active, relevant and integrated : emanation (*mūlādhāra* and *svādhisṭhāna*), preservation (*maṇipūra* and *anāhata*), and absorption (*viśuddha* and *ājña*). According to a different reckoning (*Kālī-krama*), *mūlādhāra* represents the centre of emanation (*sṛshṭichakra*), *svādhisṭhāna* the centre of preservation (*sthiti-*), *maṇipūra* the centre of absorption (*samhṛti-*), *anāhata* the centre which is unnameable (*anākhyā-*), *viśuddha* the centre illumination (*bhāsā-*) and *ājnā* the centre of final rest (*viśrāma-*).

The features of the *yantra* of *Śrī-vidyā* have been accommodated within this model. The surrounding square (*bhūpura*) and the triple girdle (*tri-vṛtta*) represent the *mūlādhāra* center (emanation, *sṛshṭi*). The sixteen-petalled lotus (*shoḍaśa-patraka*) and the eight-petalled lotus (*ashṭadaḷa*) that are outside the main pattern correspond to the *svādhishṭhāna* center (preservation, *sthiti*); they encompass the essential *yantra* and preserve it. The fourteen-cornered figure (*chaturdaśāra*), the outer and inner ten-cornered figures (*bahir-* and *antar-daśāra*) represent the *maṇipūra* center (absorption, *saṁhṛti*). The eight-cornered figure (*ashṭāra*) center at the heart. The central point (bindu) in its visible aspects represents the visuddha (*anākhyā*) center, and in its invisible aspect the *ājñā*-center or illumination (*bhāsā*). The transcendental import of the entire *yantra* is beyond the *ājñā* center stretching till the mystical thousand-petalled lotus (*sahasrāra*) on the crown of the head, which is fact is the seat of the mother-goddess.

The Samaya system prescribed the worship of the abstract Śrī-chakra in one or more of the above Worship at maṇipura will lead the devotee very near the mansion of the mother-goddess (*sārddhe*); worship at anāhata helps him get into mansion and behold the mother-goddess from a distance (*sālokya*); worship at *viśuddha* helps him approach the mother-goddess in close proximity (*sāmīpya*); worship at *ājñā* makes him acquire the same form as that of the mother-goddess (*sārūpya*). These benefits are insignificant in comparison with the absolute union with the object of the devotee's devotions at the *sahasrāra* center; it is of the nature of 'highest bliss' (*parānanda*).[11]

The bodily centers are grouped into three units or knots (*granthi*), one represented by Rudra at the *svādhishṭhāna* center, another by Vishṇu at the *anāhata* center, and the third one by Brahmā at the *ājñā* center; corresponding to the triple-girdle (*vṛtta-traya*) immediately within the surrounding square, which represents the thousand-petalled lotus. The devotee meditates the identification of this peripheral reality with the central point (the focus of Śrī-chakra).

The *viśuddha* and *ājñā* centers correspond to the 'Moon' part (*somakhaṇḍa*) of Śrī-chakra and are said to comprehend sixteen vowels of *ma*.

Muladhara and Svadhisthana together are designated by the unit-symbol *aim; manipura* and *anāhata* together by *klīm;* and *vituddha* and *ājñā* together by *sauh;* the three symbols standing for Fire, Sun and Moon respectively. They also correspond with the three aspects of sound : *paśyantī, madhyamā* and *vaikharī;* and to the three units of the *yantra* (*trikoṇa* and *ashṭakoṇa*, *daśāra-dvaya* and *chaturdaśāra, ashṭadala* and *shoḍaśa-patraka*), excluding *trivṛtta* and *bhūpura*. They further symbolize the three involvements of conscious transactions : pramāṇa (means of cognition), *pramātā* (the subject who cognizes) and *prameya* (the objects cognized); the three instruments of knowledge : individualized consciousness (*buddhi*), ego (*ahaṇkāra*) and mind (*manas*); and the three values of life : *dharma* (like according to divine law), *artha* (wealth) and *kāma* (pleasures).

From *mūlādhāra* to *viśuddha* are ten principles (five *bhūtas* : earth, water, fire air and *ākāśa;* and five *tanmātras*: smell, taste, form, sound and touch). From there till *ājñā* are eleven (five sense-organs, five organs of action, and mind). These twenty-one principles are accommodated within the main portion of Śrī-chakra (from the *bindu* to *chaturdaśāra*). Beyond this (*viz*., beyond the 'Moon'-part), is triple girdle (*trivṛtta*) and surrounding square (*bhūpura*). The four corners of *bhūpura* represent the four legs of the cot on which the pure sattva (*sadāśiva*) rests as a plank (*trivṛtta*). The four legs of the cot symbolize the four principles; *māyā* (Brahma), *śuddha-vidyā* (Vishṇu), *maheśvara* (Rudra) and *sadāśiva* (*Īśāna*). Together, the picture symbolizes twenty-five *tattvas*. The mother-goddess unites with the twenty-fifth *tattva, viz.*, Sadāśiva, and their union itself is the twenty-sixth *tattva* (*śiva-śakti-yoga*). It is this *tattva* of union that brings about, pervades and governs this entire universe of matter and spirit.[12]

The imagery of the cot on which the mother-goddess rests is symbolically significant. The four legs of the cot stand for the four principles underlying the phenomenal world : emanation (*sṛshṭi*, Brahmā), preservation (*sthiti*, Vishṇu), dissolution (*upasamhāra*, Rudra) and withdrawal of the entire world into the subtle and hidden state (*tirodhāna*, Īśvara). The plank poised over the four legs (*paryaṅka*) represents the fifth principle of the reception and retention of the withdrawn phenomena in a seedstate until the occasion for re-emanation occurs (*anugraha*, Sadāśiva). The four principles represented by the four legs are incorporated in the fifth principle in its causal condition and in the form of latency.

The five principles are said to be offsprings of the mother-goddess : Brahmā from her right eye, Vishṇu from her left eye, Rudra from her eye on the forehead, Īśvara from her navel, and Sadāśiva from her heart. The underlying symbolism is that these five deities are merely differentiated manifestations of the mother-goddess herself.

Further, *Kāmikāgama* describes the human body as the island of nine precious stones ('deho nava-ratna-dvīpah'), representing the nine *chakras* of the *yantra* of Śrī-chakra.[13] The reference is to the traditional imagery of the island of nectar-ocean (*sudhā,-sindhu*), in which the mansion of the mother-goddess (*chintāmaṇi-gṛha*) occurs, surrounded by wish fulfilling *kadaṁba*-trees. Intentions are these wish-fulfilling trees (*saṁkalpāh kalpa-taravah*) which sprout on the vast island of consciousness (individuated) and surround the inner spirit of man (*jīva*), *viz.*, the mansion of the mother-goddess.

The human body, according to the above account, has nine constituents (*dhātus*); five derived from Śakti and four from Śiva, (even as the triangles in Śrī-chakra). The constituents derived from Śakti are; skin, blood, flesh, fat and bone; those derived from Śiva are : marrow, semen, breath and vitality.[14]

3. Kāma-Kalā

The basic theme of Śrī-chakra, both in its *yantra* and in its *mantra* aspects is the recognition of the fundamental principle of all existence and experience, *kāma-kalā*. The deity of Śrī-vidyā, *viz.*, Tripura-sundarī (Lalitā, Śrī-chakra-rāja-rājeśvarī) is the personification of this principle. Kāma is a common word meaning 'desire', but its technical usage goes back to the Ṛgvedic hymn called *Nāsadīya-sūkta*.[15] Its meaning in the Vedic context as well as in the Tāntrik literature, is urge, impulsion, without an extraneous stimulation. It is the primordial, in fact original, stress in the form of movement. It is a throb (*spanda*) which brings about sound (*nāda*).

The Tāntrik ideology gives the following account. The essential reality, Śiva, is mere effulgence : consciousness without a subjective background or objective context, but containing the potentials of a transactional nature (having subject-object relations). Its phenomenal involvement begins with a surge of consciousness, prompted solely by its own nature. This is technically known as *prakāśa* ('illumination'). This initial spurt of awareness enters into the energy (*Śakti*) as actualized deliberation or immediate experience, technically called *vimarśā* (which is sometimes rendered as 'Inspiration'). The operation of the actualization is likened to the mirror reflecting the form of oneself:[16] this is the background condition for all phenomenal evolution.

Stress-involved illumination (*prakāśa*) and the deliberate and immediate actualization in experience thereof (*vimarśā*) are respectively white (pure *sattva* or contentless consciousness) and red (*rajas* or tendency towards dynamism) in colour. When the former moves in the direction of the latter, the initial 'sperm' (*bindu*) is formed which is of mixed (red and white) colour. This is the stuff of which the universe is made. When subsequently the latter moves in the direction of the former in response to the initial movement, the *bindu* swells and becomes the primordial expression or original sound (*nāda*), which is the feminine counterpart of the *bindu*. Śiva is the *bindu*, symbolized by the initial vowel *a* in the alphabet; Śakti is the *nāda* symbolized by the final consonant *ha*. Their original union is symbolized by the word *ahaṁ* (meaning 'I' providing the subjective framework for phenomenal experience).[17]

When the *bindu* and the *nāda* unite, a compound *bindu* emerges, bearing pure affinity to the male Śiva as well as the female Śakti. This represents the original impulsion being actualized, providing the possibility of a phenomenal setting. It is this that is called *Kāma*. This is a compound (*miśra*) *bindu*, without any intentionality, direction or evocative energy by itself. But it has two inseparable ingredients : a white drop representing the male factor and a red drop representing the female energy, together constituting the twin details of productive energy. Emanation is symbolized by the letter *ka*, and absorption by the letter *la*, the two being involved invariably in all phenomenal processes. Thus, this pair of drops goes by the name of *Kalā*.

The three *bindus* (the primary bindu in its isolate character, and the secondary ones in their male-female actualizations) are represented by three dots, one above and two below it, thus providing the corners of a possible triangle.

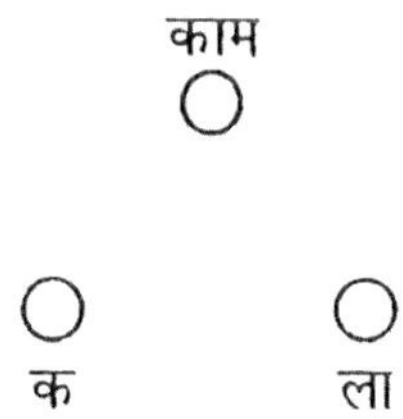

The dot on top (*bīja*) represents the unmodified nasal *ṁ* (anusvāra) in the alphabet (all the vowels comprehended), belonging to Śiva; and the two dots below (*bindu* and *nāda*) the unmodified sibilant (*visarga*), suggesting creation, emanation, projection. The top dot is Śiva, the two dots below are Śakti and *nāda* (union of Śiva and Śakti). The three dots again, represent the three fundamental powers in the entire universe, *viz.*, the original intention to manifest or *kāma*, on the part of the supreme, and intention (*icchā*) at the phenomenal level; the original awareness of this primal impulse *chit-śakti,* and phenomenal cognitions (*jñāna*); and the original action of phenomenalization, which the bindu in fact represents, and the phenomenal action (*kriyā*). Thus the three sections of *pañchadaśī* or the *yantra* of Śrī-chakra are basically involved in a triangle, called Kāma-kalā. *Kāma* is the union of Śiva (Kāmeśvara) and Śakti (Kāmeśvarī), and *kalā* is the concrete manifestation thereof.[18]

The symbolism of the three dots which together provide the main idea of a triangle, (consisting of a bent line, *vakra-rekhā*, the two ends of which are joined by a straight line, *ṛju-rekhā*) is rich and elaborate. The triangle constitutes the *kāma-kalā,* the top dot (angle) standing for 'kāma' (the primordial desire to evolve), and the two lower dots (angles) representing the actual emanation and the subsequent withdrawal. The dot representing 'kāma' is described as the source (*bīja*), an undifferentiated intention-and-actualization (*śiva-śakti, prakāśa-vimarśā*), being the preliminary condition (necessary and sufficient) for the phenomenal projection, which is figuratively known as Vāmā (literally 'that which vomits forth the phenomenal context', *vamati viśvam iti*), a goddess. The other lines emanating from the two dots, *ka* and *la*, are the twin aspects of actualization, actual emanation and final absorption, *prakāśa* (illumination) and *vimarśā* (immediate experience). The two lines are figuratively known as Jyeshṭhā (primordial nature of *mūla-prakṛti*, literally 'the first-born') and Raudrī (the goddess of dissolution or absorption). The three lines symbolize the three *guṇas* or aspects of phenomenal projection and three presiding gods : *sattva*-Brahmā, *rajas*-Vishṇu, and *tamas*-Rudra. At the apex of the triangle (*viz.*, the top dot) is placed the Sun (*sūrya*, from the root 'sū', 'to project), the right corner (or dot) is the place of Moon (*chandra*, from the root 'chadi' 'to please' and 'to nourish') and the left corner (or dot) of the Fire (*agni*, which is the Sun on earth, the principle of dissolution and absorption).[19]

Iconographically the dot on top (Brahmā) suggests the face of the mother-goddess, and the twin dots below (Hari-Hara) the breasts of the mother-goddess. *Yoginī-hṛdaya-tantra* prescribes that the devotee must contemplate on the entire triangle (*kāmakalā*) as his own body,[20] the top dot as his head and the two dots below as two sides of his body; the straight line at the base (*ṛjurekhā*) as his foundational posture (*āsana*) and the line to the left going up to the apex as his effort (*sādhanā*) and the line to the right coming down from the apex as the descent of the grace of the mother-goddess.

That the three dots actually constitute a unity (in the form of a triangle) is philosophically significant. *Śaradā-tilaka-tantra* says : "the transcendental *śakti* differentiates itself in a tripartite manner : *bindu* (point), *nāda* (sound), and *bīja* (source).

This is why the concept of 'triad' is still important in Śrī-vidyā.[21] The mother-goddess is called Tripurā.[22] and she has three forms in which she is worshipped : (1) gross or physical (*sthūla, kāyika*) in the human form, (2) subtle or verbal (*sūkshma, vāchika*) in the form of pañchadaśī or shoḍaśī or shoḍaśī; and (3) transcendental or mental (*parā, mānasa*), in the form of an abstract but all-inclusive power. In the first, she is worshipped by external riteṣ (*bahir-yāya*), either at home (for ones own benefit, *svārtha*) or in public places like temples etc., (for the food of the community, *parārtha*). In the second form, she is worshipped without external rituals but through 'inner sacrifice' (*antar-yaga*), by means of articulations of the *mantra* and meditation upon its symbolism. In the third form, the body is looked upon as the temple, and soul the mother-goddess installed in it; and worship is offered only mentally (*bhāvanā*).

There are two significant traditions the worship of Śrī-chakra current in the country. Śrī-chakra is designated as the 'yantra-in-space (*viyat-chakra*). And space is two-fold: outer (physical) space, and inner (psychic) space. Śrī-chakra is worshipped as a physical *yantra* by the group of devotees known as Kaulas. Kula' means home, community, family, village, or forest. It also means Śakti, and *akula* means Śiva; the harmonious relation between the two is styled as 'Kaula'. Whatever the meaning worship here is mainly through elaborate rituals in a community context, and to concrete representation of Tripura-Sundarī associated with the physical representation of Śrī-chakra. The earlier Kaulas worship the *yantra*, especially the primary triangle with the central point within it (*yoni*), while the later (and degenerate)

Kaulas worship the *yoni* (generative organ) of a maiden, according to Lakshmīdhara.[23]

This form of worship is regarded as inferior to the worship of Śrī-chakra at heart (inner space) resorted to by the group of devotees known as Samaya. The expression *samaya* signifies symbolism in the three-fold way : symbolism of the *yantra* (*chakra-rahasya*), symbolism of *mantra* (*pañchadaśī-rahasya*) and symbolism of worship (*pūjā-rahasya*). Worship is here carried on in ones own body, by contemplating on the harmony (*sāmya*) between the *chakras* in ones own constitution. The harmony is four-fold : correspondence between the six bodily chakras and the units of the *yantra*; correspondence between the four sides of the central point (*bindu*) and the *sahasrāra*; identity of Śiva-and-Śakti with the *bindu;* and harmony of the union of Śiva and Śakti with the devotee's body. Contemplation of these harmonies is the main procedure adopted in the Samaya worship.

This mode of worship dispenses with concrete images and external rituals. The devotee carries on contemplation on the four-fold harmony in perfect solitude, and with great austerity. The canonical basis for this worship is given as 'five auspicious scriptures' (*śubhāgama-pañchaka*), prepared by the five sage Vaśishṭha, Śuka, Sanaka, Sanandana and Sanatkumāra. This approach is recognized as proper by the Vedic tradition, which rejects the Kaula method (established by sixty-four tantras like *maya-saṁhāra*, *Yogī-nirjalā*, *Mālinī-vidyā* etc.), as 'uncivilized and lowly',[21] for they concern themselves only with physical powers and material gains and prescribe practices which are vulgar and erotic. There is also a 'mixed tradition' (*miśrakam*, containing elements from both the Kaula and the Samaya traditions), represented by a collection of eight texts (called *Chandra-kalā-vidyāshṭaka*) : *Chandra-kalā, Jyotsnāvatī, Kalānidhi, Kulārṇava, Dakshiṇāmūrti-saṁhitā, Bārhaspatyam, Bhuvaneśvarī-tantra* and *Durvāsa-mata*.

According to Lakshmī-dharam the Samaya outlook holds that the Śrī-chakra is actually identical with the moon (*chandra-maṇḍala*) located in the head of every man within the thousand-petalled lotus.[25] Flooding the entire psycho-physical constitution, the goddess, residing in this moon's orb within, enters through the central channel, Sushumnā, and sleep in the basal pit (*ādhāra-kuṇḍa*) in the form of a serpent. This is the Kuṇḍalinī-power which becomes the central theme of the Tāntrik theory and practices.[26]

Śrī-vidyā, in fact, is called 'the lore of the lunar digits' (*chandrakalā-vidyā*). The five *Saṁhitās* constituting the Samaya outlook (*śubhāgama-pañchaka*) explain in great detail how the fifteen letters of the *mantra* correspond with the fifteen digits of the moon in each fortnight commencing from the first-day (*pratipat*), when 'the moon comes out of the sun' and ending with the fifteenth day (when all the digits of the moon come out, it is the bright fortnight, and all the digits return to the sun if it is the dark fortnight). The separation of the fifteen digits of the moon from the sun is 'full-moon' (*paurṇamāsī*), and the identification of all the moon's digits in the sun is 'new-moon' (*amāvāsyā*). The sixteenth digit (*shoḍaśī-kalā* or śrī), however, is present in each of the digits, which are called 'nityās'. The Samaya worship is accorded to all the fifteen digits each day, whereas the Kaulas confine their worship to the digit that is specific to the day of the fortnight.

The digits are invoked as forms of the mother-goddess. The first digit is called Mahā-tripura-sundarī, the second

Kāmesvarī, and the third Bhagamālinī. These three together constitute the primary triangle, which is the immediate unfoldment of the central point (*bindu*), *viz.*, the mother-goddess. Other digits are called Nitya-klinnā (4th), Bheruṇḍā (5th), Vahni-vāsinī (6th), Mahā-vidyā or Vajreśvarī (7th), Raudrī (8th), Tvaritā (9th), Kula-sundarī (10th), Nīla-patākā (11th), Vijayā (12th), Sarva-maṅgalā (13th), Jvālā (14th) and Mālinī (15th). Hidden and subtle in all these digits is the *shoḍaśī* (16th), the essential source of light for all the digits : it is the *mūla-vidyā*.

These lunar digits are identified with the several aspects of the *yantra* (Śrī-chakra), and this is the characteristic feature of the *meru-prastāna*, as was mentioned earlier. They are accommodated in the petals of the sixteen-petalled lotus, as one vowel in each petal and in the eight-petalled lotus as two letters in each petal, representing the days of the fortnight. Excluding the first two (which together constitute the central point) the remaining fourteen digits are accommodated in the fourteen-angled figure. The sixteen vowels, standing for the sixteen lunar digits, are abbreviated in the letter *e* (the first part of which is 'a') and *sa* (which symbolizes the final *visarga* in the vowel group) of *pañchadaśī*. The two letters are regarded as 'vital digits' (*jīva-kalā*) and are combined to form the central point (*bindu*). The consonants beginning with *ka* and ending with *ma* are accommodated within the eight-angled figure and in the two ten-angled figures. The nine letters beginning with *ya* are accommodated (repeated twice) in the fourteen-petalled lotus, and the remaining four letters are accommodated in the four Śiva-fields. This is *kailāsa-prastāra*.

Lunar involvement is Śrī-chakra is also explained with reference to the Kuṇḍalini-lore in the *Sanathkumāra-saṁhitā* of the Samaya tradition (cf. also Lakshmī-dhara on *Saundaryalaharī* 32). The sun and the moon, presiding over the 'path of the gods' and the 'path of the ancestral spirits', move along the iḍā and piṅgalā channels in the human body, day and night, respectively. The moon, moving along the left channel, sprinkles life-giving nectar over the 72,000 ducts (nāḍi). But, the sun, moving the right channel, dries up the nectar so sprinkled. When the sun and the moon meet in 'the basal pit' (*ādhāra-kuṇḍa, mūlādhāra*) it is the new-moon (*āmāvāsyā*). All the lunar digits of the dark fortnight emerge from this source. The Kuṇḍalinī power sleeps in the 'basal pit' during the dark half of the month.

When, however, the *yogi* can keep with the help of the wind the moon in the lunar sphere and the sun in the solar sphere, the moon and the sun being arrested in their movement, become incapable of oozing out the nectar and drying it up. Then the fire from the *svādhisṭhāna* center, set ablaze by the wind in the body, dries up the store of nectar in the 'basal pit'. The Kuṇḍalinī power is thus starved, and so rises up like a serpent, pierces through the three knots (*granthi*), and entering the thousand-petalled lotus on the crown (*sahasrāra*) bites the moon that is located in the center of this lotus. The nectar the oozes out of the bitten moon, floods the lunar orb that is situated on top of the *ājñā* center (between the eye-brows). Then the entire body is flooded by the flow of nectar.

The moon's orb that is situated on top of the *ājñā* center consists of the fifteen digits (*pañchadaśa-nityāh*) of the moon. The moon that is located in the centre of the thousand-petalled lotus is the aspect of pure consciousness (*chit-kalā*), pure bliss (*ānanda-rūpa*), the very self (*ātmā*), Tripura-sundarī.

The 'basal pit' (*ādhāra*) is dense darkness (*andha-tāmisra*), the world of darkness (*miśra-loka*). So is the *maṇipūra*, which, although the seat of fire (*agni*), contains water which reflects the sun which is the previous center. The *anāhata* center (in the heart region) is a bright world (*jyotir-loka*). Above it, the *viśuddha* center (in the throat) is the lunar world (*chandraloka*) that flows from the moon. However, owing to contact with the sun, there is no moon-light in these two centers. It is only the topmost center, *viz.*, thousand-petalled lotus (on the crown of the head) that is the world of moon-light (*jyotsnā-loka*). The moon that shines there has unchanging and unfading digits (*nitya-kalā*); the lunar orb here Śrī-chakra.

In the Śrī-chakra design, the primary triangle is the 'basal pit', eight-angled figure is the *svādhisṭhāna* center, the inner ten-angled figure is the *maṇipūra* center, the outer ten-angled figure is the *anāhata* center, the fourteen-angled figure is the *viśuddha*-center, four 'male' triangles constitute the *ājñā* center, and the central point is the thousand-petalled lotus, the seat of the mother-goddess.

There are many derivative deities from the *Śrī-vidyā*. Each of the deities presiding over the nine fields of the Śrī-chakra (*chakra-nāyikā*), as well as the union-deities in the fields (*yoginī*), is given an iconographic form, a specific seed-syllable, and a ritual-placement. Three deities are regarded as significant adjuncts to the Śrī-chakra (*tripurā trividhā devī*), helping the devotee to accomplish his end while worshiping the *yantra*. They are endowed with personalities, and their own *yantras*. They receive worship as independent divinities, although in fact they are merely 'retinue spirits.'

The first of them, also the most important of the three, is called (Bālā-tripurā), She is imagined as an enchanting young maiden (*jagattritaya-mohinī*) or as a girl of sixteen (*shoḍaśī*), the mother-goddess in her juvenile condition. Those who are unable to approach Śrī-chakra directly are advised to take recourse to the worship of Bālā in her own *yantra*, given below, and through her own *mantra*, consisting of three letters (*tryaksharī*) *viz.*, *Aiṁ*, *Klīṁ*, *Sauḥ*, which is, in fact, widely employed in the worship of the mother-goddess, and the fifteen-lettered *pañchadaśī* is regarded as an evolution of the three letters, each serving as a unit (*kūṭa*) The full formular of *pañchadaśī* takes this form :

ऐं। क ए ई ल ह्रीं । क्लीं । ह स क ह ल ह्रीं ।
सौः । स क ल ह्रीं ।

and the *gāyatrī* of Śrī-vidyā is :

ऐं त्रिपुरादेवि विद्महे। क्लीं कामेश्वरी च धीमहि।
सौः तन्नः क्लिन्ना प्रचोदयात्।

The first letter (*aiṁ,* ऐं) is described as the seed of the formula (*vāgbhava*). It represents desire (*icchā*), the second letter knowledge (*jñāna*) and the third action (*kriyā*). Dakshiṇā-mūrti (the cognition oriented form of Śiva) is the *ṛshi* of this *mantra*, the *chhandas* is *paṅkti,* the *devatā* is Bālā-tripura-sundarī. The purposes of the *mantra* are to attain knowledge and literally skill, conquer the forces of evil and untimely death, and to secure prosperity.

The *yantra* of Bālā is a shortened version of Śrī-chakra, consisting of nine angles formed by the commingling of three trangles (two of Śakti and one of Śiva), surrounded by a lotus of eight petals, each of which represents a *śakti-pīṭha* (presided over by a deity : Kāma-rūpa (Subhagā), Malaya (Bhagā), Kollagiri (Kollūr) (Bhaga-sarpiṇī), Chauhāra (Bhagamālī), Kulāntaka, (Anaṅgā), Jālandahara (Anaṅgādyā-kusumā), Oḍḍiyāna (Anaṅga-mekhalā) and Koḍḍha (Anaṇga-madanā).[27] The whole pattern is enclosed within a square on which is superimposed another square so as to form an eight-cornered figure, the corners being guarded by eight divinities : Vetāla, Agni-jihvā, Kapālin, Ekapāda, Bhīma, Malaya and Hāṭaka.

Bālā is also projected as a personality : three-eyed divinity adorned with the crescent moon, youthful and brilliant like the rising sun, wearing red clothes, seated upon a pink lotus, and holding in her hands a rosary and rod. Her *dhyāna-śloka* is :

रक्ताम्बरां चन्द्रकलावतंसा
समुद्यदादित्यनिभां त्रिणेत्रां।
विद्याक्षामाजामयदामहस्तां
ध्यायामि बालां अरुणाम्बुजस्थाम्॥

The second divinity is *Mantriṇī* ('counsellor to the mother-goddess', *viz.*, the wisdom personified). She is also called Śyāmalā (dark in complexion), and Mātaṅgī (or Rāja-mātaṅgī, in her capacity to function like the gateway to Śrī-vidyā. Her *mantra* takes the following form :

ऐं क्ली सौः ऐं ह्रीं श्रीं अं,

or alternately,

ह्रीं श्री क्लीं ऐं

She symbolizes the second unit of the *pañchadaśī-mantra*, and therefore she has a formula-form :

ह्स्रैं ह स क ह ल ह्रीं ह्स्रौः

Her *yantra* is given on the next page.

She is imagined as a lady with two arms, holding the stringed instrument, *Vīṇā*, in one hand and a bowl of liquor (symbolizing the liberating bliss born out of wisdom) in the other. In this form, she is named Saṁpatpradā bhairavī ("the devotte's associate that brings all prosperity").

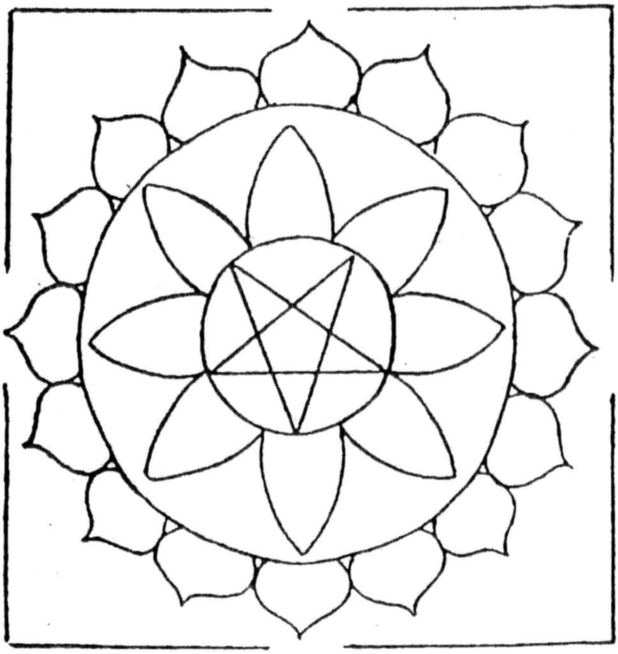

The third divinity is Daṇḍa-nāthā ('lady-commander of the forces' of the mother-goddess, symbolizing the might of *Śrī-vidyā*). She is also called Vārāhī ('the hog-faced one', or the great consumer) who destroys the evil forces that obstruct the devotee's progress, and leads ultimately to *Śrī-vidyā*. Her *mantra* is :

ऐं ग्लौं ऐं

As she represents the third unit of *pañchadaśī-mantra,* her formula form is :

स्हैं स क ल ह्रीं स्हौः

She is imagined as an eight-armed and three-eyed with the face of a hog, seated under a palmyra tree, and functioning as the trusted attendant of the goddess (*devī-chittānu-*

sāriṇī). In this form she is named Chaitanya-bhairavī ("the devotee's associate that is strength").

Still another divinity associated with Śrī-chakra is Pratyangirā, whose involvement is mainly with magic and sorcery; she is considered as a powerful repellent of the influences generated by witch-craft. In the Śrī-chakra worship, she protects the devotee against all odds, and guides him along the right path.

She is imagined as dark in complexion, terrible in aspect, riding a lion, entirely nude or wearing black garments and holding a trident. Her *mantra* is :

ओं ह्रीं नमः कृष्णवाससे शतसहस्त्रहिंसिनि
सहस्त्रवदने महाबले
अपराजिते प्रत्यङ्गिरे परसैन्यविध्वसिनि
परमन्त्रोत्सादिनि सर्वभूतदमनि

सर्वदेवान् बन्ध बन्ध, सर्वविद्याञ्छिन्दि छिन्दि, क्षोमय
क्षोमय,
परयन्त्राणि स्फोटय, स्फोटय, सर्वशृंखलांस्त्रोटय त्रोटय,
ज्वलज्ज्वालाजिह्वे करालवदने प्रत्यङ्गिरे ह्रीं नमः।

She is represented in many forms. But her significance is uniformly to drive away the hordes of enemies, sins and evil designs.

Supplementary Note on Bālā-Tripurā

The Bālā-yantra has already been mentioned. It is an important variant of Śrī-chakra, and is in vogue among numerous *sādhakas*. Some more details are, therefore, given here.

The *yantra* of Bālā-tripurā (regarded as the juvenile version of Śrī-vidyā) is a design with nine corners (*nava-yoni*) representing nine triangles (six feminine and three masculine), enclosed within an eight-petalled lotus, the whole surrounded by a square with portals on the major directions (*bhūpura*) or by two squares intersecting.

The central triangle (the seat of Bālā), which is feminine, is inscribed with the seed-syllable *Aiṁ*, the bottom triangle (also feminine) with the next syllable *Klīṁ*, and the triangle to its right (masculine) with the third seed-syllable *Sauh*. The *mantra* of Bālā (ऐं क्लीं सौः) is repeated in the same order on the other triangles. It will be seen that the three masculine triangles will contain the three male members of the *mantra*, *viz.*, *Sauh*. It will also be noted that the *mantra* occurs thrice in this delineation.

The eight petals of the lotus will contain the *gāyatrī* version of the *Bālā-mantra* :

क्लीं त्रिपुरादेवि विद्महे। कामेश्वरि धीमहि।
तन्नः क्लिन्ना प्रचेदयात्॥

The eight petals also represent the eight seats of Śakti-worship : Kāmarūpa, Malaya, Kollagiri, Chauhāra, Kulāntaka, Jālandhara, Oḍḍiyāna, and Koḍḍha; worship is conducted in these petals for the eight forms of the mother-goddess: desire (*icchā*), wisdom (*jñāna*), action (*kriyā*), desire-filled (*kāminī*), desire-fulfilling (*kāma-dāyinī*) pleasure (*rati*), pleasure-loving *(rati-priyā),* delightful (*nandā*) and maddened mind (*manonmanī*).

The surrounding square (or intersecting squares) contains the consorts that protect the devotee from harm : Tripaurāntaka, Vetāla, Agnijihvā, Kālāntaka, Kapālin, Ekapāda, Bhīma-rūpa, Malaya and Hāṭakeśvara. The guardians of the eight directions (Indra, Yama etc.) are also located on the cardinal points.

The *Bālā-mantra* has several variants. One has only three units : ह्रीं क्लीं हसौः; another has six units, the original *mantra* of three letters followed by the same letters in the reverse order : ऐं क्लीं सौः सौः क्लीं ऐं; still another has nine units : श्रीं क्लीं ह्रीं ऐं क्लीं सौः ह्रीं क्लीं श्रीं; there is also a ten-unit *mantra* called *daśārṇa* : ऐं क्लीं सौः बाला त्रिपुरे स्वाहा।

The fourteen-unit *mantra* runs thus :

ऐं क्लीं हसौः बाला त्रिपुरे सिद्धिं देहि नमः।

It includes a statement of intention. The first unit symbolises speech (*vāk*), the second desire (*kāma*) and the third the void of the sky or contentless consciousness (*vyoma*).

The seventeen-unit mantra is an expansion of this : स्क्लूीं क्ष्म्यूं ऐं त्रिपुरे सर्ववाञ्छितं देहि नमः स्वाहा। The first composite unit represents the sage Bhṛgu (*sa*), Brahmā the creator (*ka*), action (*la*), fire (*ra*), peace (*śānti, i*) and the moon (*ṁ*). The second unit includes the last letter of the alphabet (*ksha,* symbolizing the entirety of speech), fire (*ra*), the principle of destruction (*mahākāla, ma*), the serpent-energy (*kuṇḍalinī, ṛ*), Vishṇu, the preserver (*ya*), and the moon (*ṁ*). The third unit is the seed of speech (*vāg-bīja*).

Likewise, the following are other variants :

ह्रीं ह्रीं ह्रीं प्रौढत्रिपुरे आरोग्केयमैश्वर्य देहि स्वाहा
ह्रीं श्रीं क्लीं त्रिपुरा मदने सर्वं शुभं साधय स्वाहा
ह्रीं श्रीं क्लीं परापरे त्रिपुरे सर्वेप्सितं साधय स्वाहा

The iconographic representation of Bālā is given in the following hymn for contemplation. She is pictured here as a young lady red in complexion, with three eyes, adorned with moon on the head, with four hands carrying goad, noose, book and rosary :

पाशाङ्कुशौ पुस्तकमक्षसूत्रं करैदधाना सकलामरार्च्या।
रक्ता त्रिणेत्रा शशिशेखरे य ध्येयाखिर्ध्यै त्रिपुरात्र बाला।।

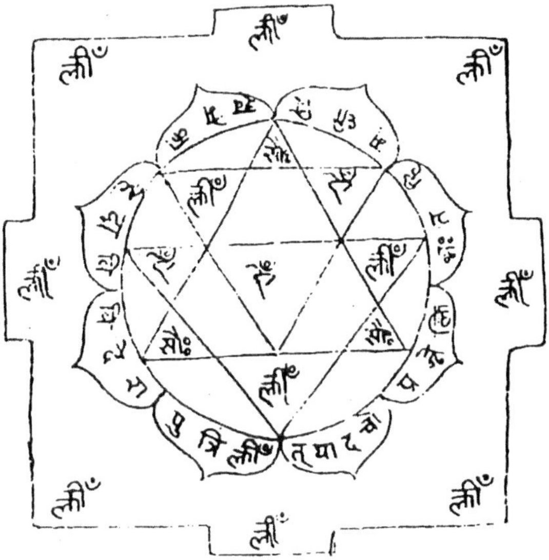

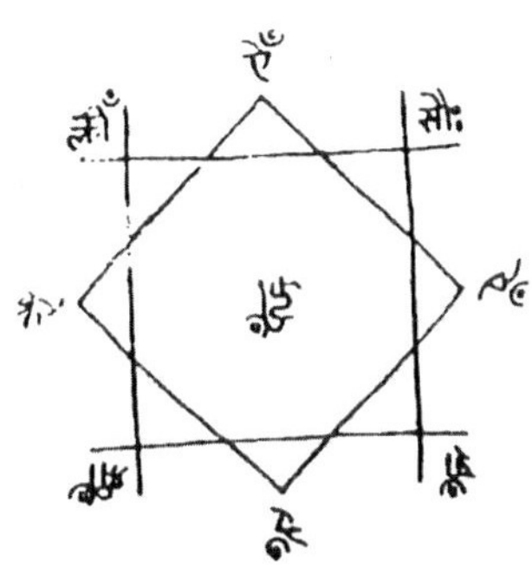

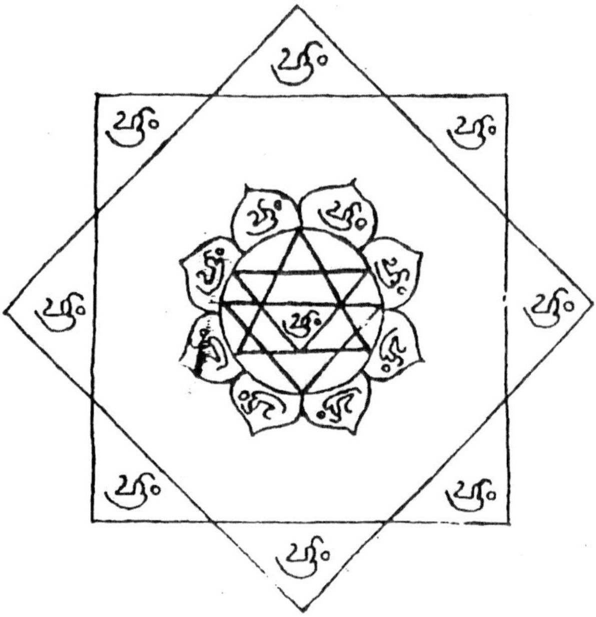

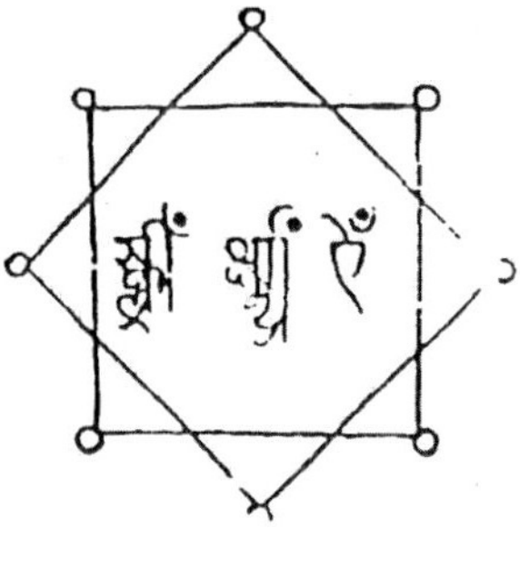

ऐं	क्लीं	सौः
सौः	क्लीं	ऐं
ऐं	क्लीं	सौः

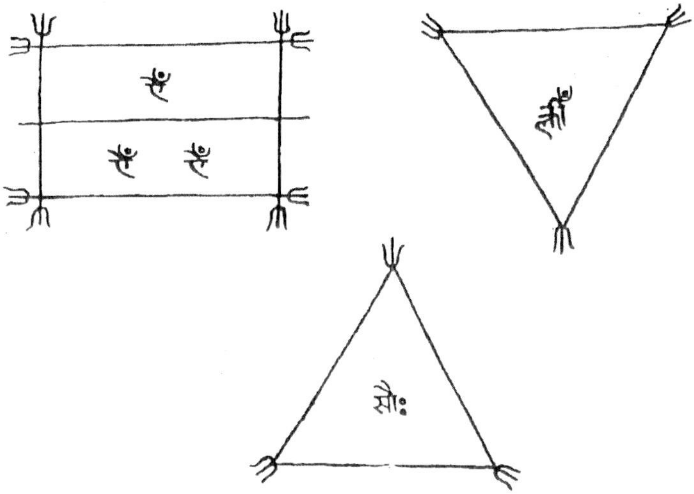

REFERENCES

1. श्रुतिश्च द्विविधा वैदिकी तान्त्रिकी चेति।

   (on *manu-samhitā*, 2, 1) also cf. *Bhāgavata 11th skandha* :

   वैदिकी तान्त्रिकी मिश्रइति त्रिविधो मखः।

   cf. also *Agni-purāṇa*, 372,34
2. चत्वार ई बिभ्रति क्षेममन्तः, RV, 5, 47,4.
3. त्र्यर्यमा मनुषो देवताता स्त्री रोचना दिव्या धारयन्त 5,29,1.
4. (ed. by J. Woodroffe : *Tantrik Text Series*, vols. 3,18 and 19; also in the *Works of Śaṁkara* Series, Vanivilas, vols, 19 and 20).
5. *Śrī-vidyārṇava-tantra*, 1, 52-60.
6. cf. *Śri-vidyārṇava-trantra*, 1, 96, 97.
7. *Ibid.*, 1, 99
8. cf. his *Tripurā-sundarī-bāhya-varivasyā*.
9. cf. his *bhāshyā* on *Bhāvanopanishat*.
10. cf. his *bhāshya* on *Kaulopanishat*.

11. *Saundarya-laharī*, verse 99, cf. Jakkaṇmātya's gloss on it. cf. also आधार स्वाधिष्ठानमणिपूरानाहतविशुद्धाज्ञाचक्रात्मक श्रीचक्रं त्रिखण्डं सोमसूर्यानलात्मकम्। एवं सोमसूर्यानला: पिण्डाण्डब्रह्माण्डे आवृत्य वर्तन्ते। पिण्डाण्ड ब्रह्मण्डयोरैक्यात् पिण्डाण्डावृतिरेव ब्रह्माण्डावृतिरिति रहस्यम्। पिण्डाण्डमतीत्य वर्तते सहस्रारकमलम्। तच्च ज्योत्स्नमयो लोक:। तत्रत्यश्चन्द्रमा नित्यकल:। षोडशकलानां षोडशनित्यात्मकत्वात्' (सुमगोदये)
(Lakshmī-dhara)

12. शिवशक्तयात्मकं सिद्धं जगदेतच्चराचर।
(चर is पिण्डाण्ड and अचर is ब्रह्माण्ड)

13. cf. *Diṇḍima-bhāshya*, on *Saundarya-laharī*, 24

14. त्वगसृङ्-मांसमेदोऽस्थिधातव: शक्तिमूलका:।
मज्जाशुक्ल प्राणिजीवधातव: शिवमूलका:।।

नवधातुरयं देहो नवयोनिसमुद्भव:।
दशमो योनिरेकैव पराशक्तिस्तदीश्वरी।।

यत्पिण्डाण्ड समुत्पन्नं तद्वद्ब्रह्माण्डमुद्भभौ।
पञ्चभूतानि शक्तनि मायादीनि शिवस्य तु।।

माया च शुद्धविद्या च महेश्वरसद शिवौ।
पञ्चविशंतित-वानि तत्रैवान्तर्भवन्ति ते।।
शिवशक्तयात्मकं विद्धि जगदेंतच्चराचरम्।। *(Kāmikāgama)*

15. *Ṛg-veda*, 10, 129

16. *Kāma-kalā-vilāsa*, 2

17. *Śiva-sūtra* :

अतोऽकारहकाराभ्यां अहमित्यपृथक्तया।
प्रपञ्चं शिवशक्तिभ्यां क्रोडीकृत्य प्रकाशते।।

also *Kāmakalā-vilāsa*,

अहङ्कारौ शिवशक्ती शून्य कारौ परस्पराश्लिष्टौ।

18. तस्य कामेश्वराख्यस्य कामेश्वर्याश्च पार्वति।
कलाख्या सविलासाख्या चख्याता कामकलेति या।।

19. रविरूपबिन्दुं मुखं कृत्वा तस्याधो दहनशीतांशू बिन्दुद्वयं स्तनयुंग कृत्वा etc. (*Saubhāgya-vardhanī,* 19)

also cf. नमोमहाबिन्दुमुखो चन्द्रसूर्यस्तनद्वयौ (*Rudra-yāmala*)

20. *Chatuh-śatī.*

बिन्दु संकल्प्य वक्त्रं तु तदधस्तात्कुचद्वयं।
तदधश्च हरार्ध तु चिन्तयेत्तदधोमुखम्।।

तत्र कामकलारूपामरुणां चिन्तयेदिह।
ततस्तनैव रूपेण निजरूपं विचिन्तयेत्।।

cf. also मुख बिन्दुतया भाति तदधस्तद् द्विबिन्दुकं।
कुचद्वयतया ज्ञेयं अधस्ताच्च त्रिकोणमिति।।

(quoted in *Tātparya-dīpini* on *Saundarya-laharī,* 19)

The expression 'harārdha' in the above verse means triangle (*yoni*) which is placed below the dots to represent the generative organ.

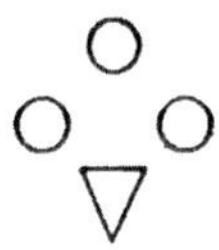

21. तिस्त्रः पुरम्त्रिपथा विश्वचर्षणी यत्राकथा अक्षरा संनिविष्टा।
आधिष्ठायैनमजरा पुराणी महत्तर महिमा देवत नाम्।।

(*Tripuropanishat*)

22. त्रिकोण मण्डल चास्याः भूपुरं च त्रिरेखक।
मन्त्रोऽपि त्र्यक्षरः प्रोक्तः तथा रूपत्रय पुनः।।

त्रिविधा कुण्डली शक्तिः त्रिदेवानां च सृष्टये।
सर्वं त्रय त्रय यस्मात्तस्मात्तु त्रिपुरा मता।। (*Kālikā-purāṇa*)

23. comm. on *Saundarya-laharī,* 41.

24. बाह्यपूजा न कर्त्तव्या कर्त्तव्या बाह्यजातिभिः।
सा क्षुद्रफलदा नृणां ऐहिकायौकसाधनात्।।

बाह्यपूजारताः कौलाः क्षपणाश्च कपालिकाः।
दिगाम्बराश्चेतिहासाः वामकास्तस्त्रवादिनः।।

अन्तराराधनपरा वैदिका ब्रह्मवादिनः।
जीवन्मुक्ता श्चरन्तयेते त्रिषु लोकेषु सर्वदा।। (*Sanat-kumāra-saṁhitā*)

समयाचारो नाम आन्तरपूजारतिः, कुलाचारो नाम बाह्यपूजारतिः इति रहस्यम् (*Lakshmīdhara's gloss on Saundarya-laharī, 8*)

25. comm. on *Saundarya-laharī*, 10.

26. *Vāmakeśvara-tantra.*

भुजङ्गाकारूपेण मूलाधारं समाश्रिता।
शक्तिः कुण्डलिनी नाम बिसतन्तुनिभाऽऽशुभा।।

(The last word, *āśubhā*, means "luminous for a moment, like lightning" *kshaṇa-prabhā vidyun-nibhā*).

27. नवयोन्यात्कं यन्त्रं बहिरष्टदलावृतं।
गृहेण पुनवर्तीतं पूजनाय लिखेत्सुधीः।।